# STUDIES IN THE CIVIL JUDICATURE OF THE ROMAN REPUBLIC

# Studies in the Civil Judicature of the Roman Republic

J. M. KELLY



OXFORD
AT THE CLARENDON PRESS
1976

*Oxford University Press, Ely House, London W.1*

GLASGOW NEW YORK TORONTO MELBOURNE WELLINGTON
CAPE TOWN IBADAN NAIROBI DAR ES SALAAM LUSAKA ADDIS ABABA
DELHI BOMBAY CALCUTTA MADRAS KARACHI DACCA
KUALA LUMPUR SINGAPORE HONG KONG TOKYO

ISBN 0 19 825337 0



*Printed in Great Britain*
*at the University Press, Oxford*
*by Vivian Ridler*
*Printer to the University*

# PREFACE

I WOULD like to acknowledge here, with deep gratitude, the very considerable help I received from Professor Wolfgang Kunkel of Munich, Professor Max Kaser of Salzburg, and Mr. J. A. Crook, President of St. John's College, Cambridge, who read the entire manuscript and went to extraordinary pains in making suggestions for its improvement. My best thanks are due also to the Deutscher Akademischer Austauschdienst, whose very generous support made possible for me several quiet weeks of study at the Institut für geschichtliche Rechtswissenschaft in Heidelberg, to whose Director, Professor Karl-Heinz Misera, I am deeply obliged for an unfailingly kind and helpful reception.

Lastly, I would like to mention with sincere gratitude my friends Dr. and Mrs. William Hayes of Oxford, and Dr. and Mrs. Heinz Miess of Mannheim, whose extraordinary generosity and hospitality turned into positive holidays my sojourns in England and Germany in search of books not easily available in Dublin.

J. M. KELLY

*University College, Dublin*
*January 1975*

# CONTENTS


| | | |
|---|---|---|
| | Abbreviations | viii |
| I. | The *Centumviri* | 1 |
| II. | The Jurisdiction of *Recuperatores* | 40 |
| III. | The Statistics of Roman Litigation | 71 |
| IV. | 'Loss of Face' as a Factor Inhibiting Litigation | 93 |
| V. | The *Unus Iudex* | 112 |
| | Conclusion | 134 |
| | Index of sources | 137 |
| | Index of contents | 141 |

# ABBREVIATIONS

| | |
|---|---|
| Behrends, *Geschworenenverfassung* | Okko Behrends, *Die römische Geschworenenverfassung*, Göttinger Rechtswissenschaftliche Studien, Bd. 80; Göttingen, 1970. |
| Kaser, *RPR* | Max Kaser, *Das römische Privatrecht*, i (2nd edition); Munich, 1971. |
| Kaser, *RZPrR* | Max Kaser, *Das römische Zivilprozessrecht*; Munich, 1966. |
| Kunkel, *Kriminalverfahren* | Wolfgang Kunkel, *Untersuchungen zur Entwicklung des römischen Kriminalverfahrens in vorsullanischer Zeit*, Abhandlungen der bayerischen Akademie der Wissenschaften (Phil.-hist. Klasse, Heft 56); Munich, 1962. |
| *RE* | Pauly-Wissowa, *Realenzyklopädie der classischen Altertumswissenschaft*. |
| Schmidlin, *Rekuperatorenverfahren* | Bruno Schmidlin, *Das Rekuperatorenverfahren: eine Studie zum römischen Prozess*, Arbeiten aus dem juristischen Seminar d. Universität Freiburg/Schweiz; Freiburg, 1963. |
| *VIR* | *Vocabularium Iurisprudentiae Romanae*; Berlin, 1894–. |
| Watson, *Persons* | Alan Watson, *The Law of Persons in the Later Roman Republic*; Oxford, 1967. |
| Watson, *Property* | Alan Watson, *The Law of Property in the Later Roman Republic*; Oxford, 1969. |
| Watson, *Succession* | Alan Watson, *The Law of Succession in the Later Roman Republic*; Oxford, 1971. |
| *ZSS* | *Zeitschrift der Savigny-Stiftung für Rechtsgeschichte (Romanistische Abteilung)*. |

# I

# The *Centumviri*

THE purpose of these essays is to present the different parts of the civil judicature of the Roman Republic in such a way as to give reasons for their separate existence.

The types of judicial instance which are evidenced in the Roman sources are strikingly different from each other in mode of composition and, in large measure, in their spheres of competence. While this fact is naturally recognized and documented in the many textbooks and monographs on Roman civil procedure, and explanations sometimes given for the origin of individual jurisdictions, there has not yet appeared a complete and organic account of the coexistence of several jurisdictions with an adequate explanation of the social or political or legal reasons behind their special characteristics.

Two examples of this lack—one from the major modern textbook, one from a fairly recent and striking monograph—will sufficiently make this point. Kaser's *Römisches Zivilprozessrecht*, published in 1966, describes in consecutive sections[1] the functions of the *centumviri* and *decemviri*, so far as they are known, in the *legis actio* period; then the function of the single judge (*iudex* or *arbiter*); but with no discussion of why, in some kinds of case, a collegiate rather than a one-judge court was used, or vice versa; and this treatment is repeated later in the section on the judges of the formulary procedure.[2] The *centumviri* and *decemviri* survived into this age, and this survival might seem in need of explanation, but none is offered. Kaser, it is true, does offer a reason for the special jurisdiction of the *recuperatores*,[3] but the addition of this jurisdiction—already well in existence, incidentally, before the formulary procedure became generally

[1] 37 ff. [2] 138 ff.
[3] 142–3; following Schmidlin, *Rekuperatorenverfahren*.

established—only intensifies the need to give an orderly account of the factors which, for example in the age of Cicero, had produced the coexistence of *unus iudex*, *recuperatores*, and *centumviri*.

The more recent monograph of Okko Behrends, *Die römische Geschworenenverfassung* (1970), might have raised, through its title, an expectation that this question would be faced and answered, but this does not happen. The author's main theme is his view of the mechanism—in particular the timing—of the Roman judicial engine, and all the problems of the total, variegated Roman judicature are subordinated to, and somewhat obscured by, the presentation of the *unus iudex* as the central and original figure—something which is itself problematical—and by treating all the other jurisdictions in a series of short sections as subsidiary phenomena ('Die Richter neben dem *iudex unus*'). Behrends does indicate possible justifications for them individually, but they seem inadequate to explain the total judicial structure whose very variety is its most conspicuous feature.

Any particular approach to this theme may be open to objection on the grounds of method, but it seems to me defensible to take as a starting-point the two jurisdictions which exhibit the strongest mutual contrast in point of composition and procedure: the *unus iudex* and the *centumviri*. If it is possible to isolate factors which explain the latter, these very same factors will throw light, by their absence, on the nature of the former. If we then add a consideration of the third main jurisdiction in the period, that of *recuperatores*, and can find special factors here too, this will round out and nearly complete our understanding of the *unus iudex* as a social no less than a legal phenomenon.

The first knot to be disentangled is accordingly the nature of, and the reasons for, the centumviral jurisdiction. This jurisdiction has been for many years a subject of controversy, partly on account of the difficulty of delimiting its competence with certainty, partly on the question of its antiquity; and these matters concerning its external nature must be discussed before trying to elucidate the reason for the court's existence in the first place.

Perhaps even a prior question is that of the composition of the court. The name *centumviri* implies that it consisted of 100 members. Yet the only texts which give clear information on the size of the court mention numbers of which neither is exactly 100.

Festus[1] reports that the court in fact consisted of 105 members, a number reached by the election of three members each by the thirty-five *tribus*. This slight numerical discordance need not throw doubt on the mode of composition reported by Festus, because Festus himself describes the name *centumviri* as one of convenience, and moreover we have the express testimony of Varro[2] that a conventional number need not be exactly used in practice; to illustrate this he points out that we do not mean it literally when we speak of the thousand ships that sailed to Troy or of the hundred-man court at Rome (*sic numerus non est ut sit ad amussim, ut non est, cum dicimus mille naves isse ad Troiam, centumvirale esse iudicium Romae*).

La Rosa[3] believes that the court of the *centumviri* was originally identical with the primitive Roman Senate of 100, and is therefore obliged to get rid somehow of the evidence of Festus. Her attempt in this direction is two-pronged. Firstly, she objects that if the original court in fact contained 105, and not 100 members (as Festus implies) it would not have been called *centumviri* at all. The Romans, she points out, could be exact in such a context, and she instances the XXVIvirate. She suggests that if in fact at some stage the court was reformed and enlarged to 105, the original name of *centumviri* might well have been *retained* for reasons of convenience. But she does not consider what might have motivated such a numerically trivial increase, nor the form which this reformation might have taken. Another consideration which must weaken La Rosa's objection is this: the word *centuria* was used in the Republic in at least three

[1] Paul. ex Fest. 54 (Mueller). Kunkel (*Kriminalverfahren*, 118 n.) thinks this text is certainly abbreviated from the original, and possibly also distorted.

[2] *Res rusticae* 2. 1. 26.

[3] 4 *Labeo* (1958) 14 ff., 34.

different senses (a voting unit, a military unit, and a division of a trade-guild),[1] but it is highly unlikely that in any one of these senses it could ever have been meant to mean a collection of exactly one hundred persons. La Rosa's argument based on the numerical discordance is, therefore, insufficient to invalidate Festus' report of the *centumviri* being an elected body formed from the *tribus*; though Kunkel[2] is ready to assume that the *centumviri* need not necessarily from the beginning have consisted of the same number of members, and of course, even assuming election from the *tribus*, the number of members per tribe must have been correspondingly greater at the time when there were fewer *tribus* than the 35 mentioned by Festus.

La Rosa's other argument against the *tribus*-election system is at first sight more substantial. It is this: if (as she holds)[3] the *centumviri* were an archaic judicial organ, going back to the earliest period of Rome's history, then it must be wrong to suggest that the members were elected by the *tribus*, because this would have given both plebeians and patricians a voice in the election, and this she finds a democratic element which seems, in relation to an archaic period, to be an anachronism. (Her own theory, whereby the *centumviri* were originally simply the Senate, meets no such difficulty.) But perhaps the difficulty is exaggerated. Even though power and influence played a great part in the practical working of the Republican constitution, it was still substantially a democracy. If there was no obstacle to the plebeians taking part in the various *comitia*—even though they could not, at first, occupy the magistracies whose incumbents presided over them—it is hard to see anything which would *a priori* exclude the possibility of a court of 100 being formed on a similar footing.

Apart from this general consideration, it may be appropriate to mention here the theory of Kunkel[4] that the composition of the court from as wide a base as possible—viz. from all the *tribus*—may have served the purpose of spreading responsibility for the court's decisions as thinly as possible among as many

[1] *RE* 3. 1952 ff. (Kübler, v. Domaszewski).

[2] *Kriminalverfahren*, 118.

[3] Op. cit. 29.

[4] Op. cit. 119.

different groups as possible, thus making it difficult for the defeated party or his supporters to commit acts of revenge on the judicial organ responsible for his defeat. Looked at in the light of this (admittedly unprovable) theory, the inclusion of plebeians as well as patricians in the court would become even more natural, since the 'division of responsibility' motive would be better served the wider the political and social spectrum of the court's membership.

Accordingly, it seems best to stick for the moment to the association of the *centumviri* with the *tribus*; and, as will be seen, this very association may provide a valuable hint of the *raison d'être* of the court itself.

Opinions on the date of the court's origin have been very divided. Among the earlier writers, of whom Bethmann-Hollweg[1] may serve as an example, the *centumviri* were regarded as a most ancient institution. A reaction against this point of view set in with Francesca Bozza;[2] her main objection to the thesis that the *centumviri* had a very early origin is based on the *argumentum ex silentio* that they are nowhere mentioned in early Republican sources, whether legal or secular. The XII Tables, however, do not describe the composition of the Roman judicature, but take it for granted; and the occasional reference to *iudex* might as easily be interpreted as applying to a member of the *centumviri* as to any other judicial organ, e.g. the rule providing the death penalty for a judge who takes bribes.[3] Bozza further argues that in Plautus *Men.* 580 ff., where (she says) the various Roman judicial organs are enumerated, the *centumviri*, had they existed, ought to have been mentioned, but Plautus does not mention them. This argument is of no force at all. The passage in question deals with swindling, and reads:

Qui neque leges neque aequom bonum usque colunt,
  Sollicitos patronos habent.
Datum denegant quod datum est, litium pleni, rapaces
  Viri, fraudulenti,

[1] *Der römische Civilprocess*, i. 56 ff.
[2] *Sulla competenza dei centumviri* (1928).
[3] Aulus Gellius, *Noctes Atticae* 20. 1. 7.

Qui aut faenore aut periuriis habent rem paratam,
Mens est in quo lis est.
Eis ubi dicitur dies, simul patronis dicitur,
[Quippe qui pro illis loquantur, qui male fecerint;]
Aut ad populum aut in iure aut apud aedilem res est.

A matter of this kind would not, on any hypothesis of the competence of the *centumviri*,[1] have come before their court. If, in fact, Plautus *had* mentioned the *centumviri* here, it would have been more than strange.

As against these negative considerations, two more recent writers—La Rosa[2] and Kunkel[3]—have returned to the standpoint of Bethmann-Hollweg, and have decided in favour of a very early date for the *centumviri*, in my view rightly. Both of them regard as significant the fact that the procedure used in centumviral litigation was always the *legis actio*.[4] Bozza assigns the origin of the *centumviri* to the late second century B.C., and La Rosa and Kunkel naturally find it incredible that, just at the time when the *legis actio* was beginning to give way to the formulary system, a new court could have been created to which this obsolescent procedure was attached for good. On the contrary, the association of *legis actio* with *centumviri* must point to a more ancient origin; and indeed the well-known passage of Aulus Gellius on the mysterious *lex Aebutia*[5] might well suggest that the centumviral jurisdiction, even if not mentioned in the surviving fragments of the XII Tables, does in fact go back to that statute or beyond it: *omnisque illa duodecim tabularum antiquitas, nisi in legis actionibus centumviralium causarum lege Aebutia lata consopita est.* A plausible, even if not a necessary interpretation of this passage might see it as implying that the *legis actio* procedure in centumviral cases was in fact prescribed, implicitly if not expressly, by the XII Tables themselves, and that the *centumviri* were therefore of at least that age.

[1] i.e. even on the broadest interpretation of Cicero, *De oratore* 1. 173 (to be discussed below, pp. 9 ff.); the passage in question omits all reference to the whole law of contract and delict.

[2] Op. cit.

[3] Op. cit. 115 ff.

[4] Gaius, *Inst.* 4. 31, 95; Gellius, *N.A.*, 16. 10. 8.

[5] Loc. cit.

Kunkel draws[1] a further and, for him, confirmatory argument from the research of Alföldi,[2] which goes to show that the spear (*hasta*)[3] customarily set up at sittings of the *centumviri*, and which is often used in literature as a metaphor for the court itself, was an extremely archaic symbol of state power. He concludes that the *centumviri* must be assigned to the earliest phase of the Roman state, but accepts the possibility that the court known in historical times as that of the *centumviri* may originally have borne some quite different name.[4]

Behrends,[5] more recently, returns to the theory which sees in the *centumviri* a relatively modern innovation. His main objection to Kunkel's view seems of small substance. According to him, the *centumviri* can hardly be earlier than 241 B.C., because before that date there were only 33, not 35 *tribus*, so that with three members from each tribe one would be left with only 99 judges, which he thinks less likely to have carried the title *centumviri* than 105. Apart from the fact that the passage from Varro cited above would be an answer just as cogent for 99 as for 105, there is the additional possibility that if one counts the presiding magistrate as well, one gets an exact 100 even before 241 B.C. Moreover, Behrends's argument gets no stronger through being applied to even earlier periods, since no matter how small the number of *tribus* in existence at any time, some multiple (if not 3, then 4 or 5 or 6) will produce roughly 100.

What is essential in the report of Festus is not the arithmetic,

[1] Op. cit. 117.

[2] 63 *Am. J. Arch.* (1959) 1 ff. Alföldi's conclusions are rejected by Behrends, op. cit. 104 n. 64.

[3] Gaius, *Inst.* 4. 16.

[4] J. A. Crook has privately commented on the failure of Gaius to list *centumviralia iudicia* among the *iudicia legitima*; this, he thinks, must tell against the extreme antiquity of the court. But if Gaius does not describe the *centumviralia iudicia* as *legitima*, neither does he list them as *imperio continentia*. It is true that, on the definition of *iudicium legitimum* in Gaius 4. 104, a *iudicium centumvirale* ought, by exclusion, to rank as *imperio continens*; yet in the definition of *iudicium imperio continens* in the very next section, the *centumviri* are not mentioned. It seems to me that this question is best dealt with by saying that the distinction *legitimum/imperio continens* is being described here by Gaius only in the context of the formulary system; he has previously disposed of the *legis actiones*, to which procedural world the *centumviri* belong. See Kaser, *RZPrR* 116 n. 76; Broggini, *Iudex Arbiterve* 211.

[5] Op. cit. 103 ff.

but the concept of a large court deliberately representative of subdivisions of the people.[1]

Equally controversial with the question of the date of the court's origin is the question of its competence; but the latter is of perhaps greatest importance in approaching the social reasons for the court's existence at all. There is, however, at least one point at which the questions of date of origin and of competence overlap; this is a consequence of Bozza's theory[2] that the *centumviri* were formed as a court as a direct consequence of the rise of freedom of testamentary disposition, which theory, if correct, would place the court's emergence in the later rather than in the earlier Republic. Perhaps this had better be cleared out of the way before we consider the question of competence from the beginning.

According to Bozza, with freedom of testamentary disposition litigation about wills became so frequent, and cases became so full of incidental questions of importance, that they could not be left to a single judge. Admittedly there is no trace of the *unus iudex* in succession cases in the Republic. But Bozza's theory, apart from its lack of positive supporting evidence, that the volume and importance of succession cases suddenly justified their removal (presumably) from the field of the *unus iudex* to that of a court with 100 members, is unconvincing. Were there not plenty of *iudicia privata*—arising e.g. from contracts between large capitalists and merchants—whose 'importance' might have justified the same step? She explains that the state must have intervened, by creating the *centumviri* as an exception from the general regime of the *unus iudex*, in order to put an end to corruption. But it is impossible to accept the implication that corruption was necessarily more widespread or more dangerous in succession cases than in others; and, while obviously it is harder to bribe 100 judges than to bribe a single one, collegiate courts were not immune to the influence of money or power, as the history of the *quaestiones* towards the end of the Republic fully demonstrates.[3] Bozza's view on the motive behind the

[1] Festus, loc. cit.
[2] Op. cit. 15–16.
[3] Kelly, *Roman Litigation*, 33 ff.

creation of the *centumviri* thus adds nothing to her view on the date of their origin; and no other author has ventured an opinion on this question, vital though it might seem to any hypothesis which would place this origin any later than the beginnings of the Roman legal order, i.e. which would regard the creation of the centumviral jurisdiction as a reformation or innovation.

On the competence of the court, there is a wide variety of opinion. At one extreme, Bozza believes[1] that the *centumviri* had a jurisdiction which was absolutely limited to questions of succession; at the other extreme, Wlassak[2] was led by the apparent identity of the *hasta* with the *festuca* to speak of a general competence in *vindicationes*. Kunkel[3] and Kaser[4] occupy intermediate positions.

The most important text in this connection, and the one which has been given the most diverse interpretations, is Cicero *De orat.* 1. 173. It is a passage in which Cicero comments on the impertinence of inexperienced and ignorant orators, who have the presumption to appear and plead in different courts, particularly that of the *centumviri*, in which a huge range of legal institutions may be in issue:

Nam volitare in foro, haerere in iure ac praetorum tribunalibus, iudicia privata magnarum rerum obire, in quibus saepe non de facto, sed de aequitate ac iure certetur, iactare se in causis centumviralibus, in quibus usucapionum, tutelarum, gentilitatum, agnationum, alluvionum, circumluvionum, nexorum, mancipiorum, parietum, luminum, stillicidiorum, testamentorum ruptorum aut ratorum, ceterarumque rerum innumerabilium iura versentur, cum omnino, quid suum, quid alienum, quare denique civis aut peregrinus, servus aut liber quispiam sit, ignoret, insignis est impudentiae.

Anyone coming fresh to this text, knowing that virtually all the centumviral cases mentioned in Roman literature are (where

[1] Op. cit. 24 ff.

[2] *RE* 3. 1940 ff.

[3] Op. cit. 119 n. 437; he believes that the court handled other *vindicationes*, particularly those concerning ownership of land, as well as those arising in inheritance disputes.

[4] Op. cit. 38–9; he thinks the court's competence extended to the *hereditatis petitio*, the *querela inofficiosi testamenti*, *vindicatio* of land, and certain disputes about status.

the subject-matter is clear beyond doubt) in fact succession cases of one kind or another, would assume at once that the *centumviri* had a very wide competence indeed, and might conclude that any dispute arising from the various matters enumerated was automatically and generally within the centumviral jurisdiction. Bozza, however, argued[1] that the passage is perfectly consistent with the restriction of the centumviral jurisdiction to inheritance cases only.

She reached this position by, first of all, consigning the words *cum omnino...ignoret* to a footnote, with the explanation that they were no more than a general measure of legal ignorance, equally applicable to the *in iure* and *iudicia privata* parts of the passage (a view shared by Behrends),[2] and, secondly, arguing that every one of the other matters mentioned after *in causis centumviralibus*—*usucapio*, *adluvio* etc.—occurs in the text only to denote questions which might arise in a preliminary or marginal way in the course of an action about an inheritance. Thus, according to her, if Cicero mentions a servitude in the context of the *centumviri*, it is only because a dispute over an inheritance can require the investigation of such matters, e.g. in order to establish just what does belong to the inheritance.

Her method was to take, one by one, the areas in which Wlassak had asserted a centumviral competence (apart from inheritance cases) and demonstrate that the evidence in each area is extremely thin; and in my view, despite the critical review of her thesis by Koschaker[3] and the carefully weighed judgment of Kaser,[4] she was in the right.

Both Wlassak and Kaser think a centumviral jurisdiction existed in litigation purely about status—in the main, *causae liberales* would be here in question. Yet the texts on which this conclusion rests will not, in my opinion, support it. There is, for instance, the combined weight of Cicero *De orat.* 1. 181 and 238; the former passage adverts to the case of one Mancinus, whose revived citizenship through *postliminium* was denied by P. Rutilius, a *tribunus plebis*, and Mancinus' situation is used by Cicero to illustrate the statement that *capitis nostri saepe potest*

[1] Loc. cit. [2] Op cit. 106 n. 69. [3] 50 *ZSS* (1930) 679 ff. [4] Loc. cit.

*accidere ut causae versentur in iure*. In the latter passage, Cicero comes back to the same case, this time saying it had been one of the *maximae centumvirales causae*. Bozza's objection to treating the case as evidence of jurisdiction in cases where status, and no more, was in issue is that, so far as the text goes, the determination of Mancinus' status might quite easily have been incidental to a question of inheritance, and indeed, as I hope to show later, such a problem was all too likely to be a component of an issue which primarily was one of succession. This consideration, moreover, is quite independent of the further difficulty that a well-established jurisdiction in *causae liberales* as such already existed and was vested in *decemviri*,[1] so that to take these passages as proving a status competence, independent of inheritance questions, on the part of the *centumviri* introduces the complication of a concurrence of jurisdictions, which in turn would call for explanation.

According to Wlassak,[2] further evidence of centumviral competence in *causae liberales* is provided by two Digest passages, D. 42. 1. 38 (Paulus) and D. 40. 1. 24. pr. (Hermogenianus). The former reads: *Inter pares numero iudices si dissonae sententiae proferantur, in liberalibus quidem causis, secundum quod a divo Pio constitutum est, pro libertate statutum optinet, in aliis autem causis pro reo.* The latter: *Lege Iunia Petronia, si dissonantes pares iudicum existant sententiae, pro libertate pronuntiari iussum.* Bozza[3] denies that either of these texts shows a centumviral competence in *causae liberales*, her reason being that if either the centumviral court consisted of 105 members, or one of its divisions consisted of 45 members,[4] the envisaged situation of an even number of votes on each side could not result; accordingly, the *iudices* in question here must be some body other than the *centumviri*. This argument is not very strong, as Koschaker[5] pointed out; we have no really firm information on the size of the divisions in which the *centumviri* may have sat, and, if these divisions themselves were at all numerous, as the assignation of *decemviri* to them as presidents might

[1] See below, pp. 67 ff. [2] Loc. cit. [3] Op. cit. 62.

[4] This is implied by Pliny's reference (*Ep.* 6. 33. 3) to a joint session of four *consilia* making up a centumviral court of 180 members.

[5] Op. cit. 685–6.

hint,[1] it is not at all certain that a division might not have contained an even number of judges. I would go even further than Koschaker in another point; he says that if a judge dropped out, through illness for example, from an uneven-number court, the uneven number might be restored by the magistrate adding a substitute; but I am not sure if there is any evidence that the Romans attached importance to numerical exactness in dealing with a large body of judges. For example, there is no evidence that a *quaestio*-trial depended on a particular number of judges both hearing and voting on the issue. The real answer, in my opinion, to the argument built by Wlassak on these texts is provided, as Marrone has pointed out,[2] by a Digest passage almost immediately preceding D. 42. 1. 38 and clearly belonging to the same passage from Paulus l. xvii *ad edictum*:

D. 42. 1. 36: Pomponius libro XXVII ad edictum scribit, si uni ex pluribus iudicibus de liberali causa cognoscenti de re non liqueat, ceteri autem consentiant, si is iuraverit sibi non liquere, eo quiescente ceteros, qui consentiant, sententiam proferre, quia, etsi dissentiret, plurium sententia optineret.

This passage shows one of a number of judges withholding his vote on the ground *non liquet*, and says that, if the other judges are unanimous, their judgment will hold good because they might have outvoted him even if he had differed from them. There is no word of the silent judge being replaced and the issue tried again in what must have been an equally common situation, namely that the remaining judges were *not* unanimous; on the contrary, Paulus goes straight on to envisage firstly, that the dropping-out of the doubtful judge leaves an even number of judges behind, and secondly, that if this even number is divided in a *liberalis causa*, at any rate, the *favor libertatis* will make that half of the court prevail. The result of all this is that the *centumviri* have no reason to be considered in this context at all, because the passage may just as easily, and more naturally (given their established jurisdiction in *causae liberales*) apply to a board of *recuperatores*.

[1] Pomp. D. 1. 2. 2. 29; see below, p. 67.

[2] 24 *Annali del seminario giuridico dell'Università di Palermo* (1955), 30.

A further passage used by Wlassak[1] to show centumviral jurisdiction in *causae liberales* is D. 40. 12. 30; absolutely nothing in the text, however, could possibly raise such an idea except for the plurality of judges in the phrase *cogi iudices*, which, even if genuine and not interpolated as has been suspected, could again be more naturally taken as referring to *recuperatores*. On the uselessness of this passage to prove Wlassak's point I agree with Bozza[2] and Marrone.[3]

In the result, it seems to me that the case for the *centumviri* having had a jurisdiction in *causae liberales* is not proven, and that the strong likelihood is that they had not, though certainly they were called on to decide questions of status, including questions of liberty, in the course of litigation about inheritance.

Wlassak,[4] followed by Kaser,[5] also thought that the *centumviri* exercised jurisdiction in disputes about the ownership of land. According to Kaser, this is shown to be a centumviral matter by the existence of the *exceptio quod praeiudicium praedio non fiat* for which he cites Africanus D. 44. 1. 16, 18 together with certain modern authors. I confess I cannot see the point of this contention, as the text does not appear to support it in any way, nor do the authors he mentions. The text reads as follows:

16 Fundum Titianum possides, de cuius proprietate inter me et te controversia est, et dico praeterea viam ad eum per fundum Sempronianum, quem tuum esse constat, deberi. Si viam petam, exceptionem 'quod praeiudicium praedio non fiat' utilem tibi fore putavit, videlicet quod non aliter viam mihi deberi probaturus sim, quam prius probaverim fundum Titianum meum esse.

18 Fundi, quem tu proprium tuum esse dicis, partem a te peto et volo simul iudicio quoque communi dividundo agere sub eodem iudice; item si eius fundi, quem tu possideas et ego proprium meum esse dicam, fructus condicere tibi velim: quaesitum est an exceptio 'quod praeiudicium fundo partive eius non fiat' obstet an denegenda est. Et utrubique putat intervenire praetorem debere nec permittere petitori, priusquam de proprietate constet, huiusmodi iudiciis experiri.

The sense of the passages is plain, but their bearing on the *centumviri* not evident, to me at least. Why should an action on

[1] Loc. cit. [2] Op. cit. 37, 63–4. [3] Op. cit. 313 ff.
[4] Loc. cit. [5] Op. cit. 39 n. 27.

the ownership issues not have taken place before an *unus iudex*, complete with the *exceptio* envisaged? Other texts supposed to show centumviral jurisdiction in this field are Cicero *De orat.* 1. 173, to which I shall shortly return, and Gaius *Inst.* 4. 16, 95. Their value for this purpose is denied by Bozza[1] and Marrone;[2] and, whatever one makes of the Cicero passage, those from Gaius are impossibly weak supports for the Wlassak/Kaser position. The former contains a purely parenthetical reference to the *centumviri* (occasioned by a reference to *hasta* = *festuca* in the *legis actio sacramento in rem*); the latter can perfectly easily be read as relating to the *vindicatio* of an inheritance. On top of this, none of the several centumviral trials mentioned in lay literature are ordinary disputes about ownership.

There remains the field of inheritance cases, and here, by contrast with *causae liberales* and *vindicationes*, so far from there being any need to strain ingenuity and credulity in order to establish a centumviral jurisdiction, the jurisdiction is clear and manifest beyond any doubt, and the passages which show the *centumviri* hearing *hereditatis petitiones* and the *querela inofficiosi testamenti* are so numerous and so unambiguous that they do not need recital in the text.[3] Armed with the knowledge of this contrast, if we recur now to Cicero *De orat.* 1. 173 it seems to me impossible to resist Bozza's conclusion that the various matters mentioned in the culminating part of this passage are matters not in themselves all capable of being litigated before the *centumviri*, but rather matters likely to be involved in centumviral litigation about inheritance disputes.[4] It may be remarked

[1] Op. cit. 24 ff., 31–2.

[2] Op. cit. 28 f.

[3] e.g.: D. 5. 2. 13; 5. 2. 17. pr.; Cic. *Brut.* 144, 197; *De leg. agr.* 2. 44; Val. Max. 7. 7. 1, 7. 7. 2; Pliny *Ep.* 5. 1. 7; Phaedrus *Fab.* 3. 10; Quint. *Inst. or.* 3. 10. 3, 4. 2. 5, 7. 4. 20; Hier. *Ep.* 50. 2.

[4] J. A. Crook privately comments that he is not convinced that the matters recited in *De orat.* 1. 173 are merely preliminary questions in inheritance cases, and asks: how can *parietum, luminum, stillicidiorum* be got under this head? There is no need to regard them as 'preliminary'; Cicero's point probably is that an orator arguing a case before *centumviri* might well need to know the law on these matters which could be relevant to an inheritance case. I can, for instance, easily imagine that a grievance based on testamentary dispositions in regard to urban servitudes or the like could be an element in the *querela inofficiosi testamenti*. For examples of *lumina* and *stillicidia* in the context of trouble about a will, see D. 8. 2. 10;

that one of the elements of the passage most likely to lead one to a wrong conclusion is the final *cum omnino quid suum, quid alienum, quare denique civis aut peregrinus, servus aut liber quispiam sit, ignoret*; if one attaches this description of legal ignorance merely to the immediately preceding picture of matters commonly in issue in centumviral cases, obviously both *vindicationes* and status cases seem to be attributed to the *centumviri;* but, as Behrends[1] rightly points out, these words are intended to describe all legally ignorant orators whether acting *in iure*, in *iudicia privata*, or in the *centumvirales causae*, all of which are mentioned in the passage taken as an entirety.

Two further questions must be got out of the way before we approach the heart of our problem, the *raison d'être* of the centumviral jurisdiction in inheritance cases. The first question is whether this jurisdiction was exercised concurrently with that of the *unus iudex;* the second, whether there was any qualification, in terms of a lower limit of money value involved, on the centumviral jurisdiction. It will be observed that there is a certain interdependence between these two questions, because if the *unus iudex* is excluded from inheritance litigation, clearly there is no one left to judge disputes about estates of small value; while conversely if it is established that the *centumviri* decided cases only where the subject-matter had a certain minimum value, estates of less than that value must have been litigated before a simpler court, and nothing but the *unus iudex* seems to be a possibility here.

The evidence for the operation of an *unus iudex* in *hereditatis petitio* or *querela inofficiosi testamenti* in the Republic or early Empire is next to non-existent. The only text cited in this sense (apart from D. 5. 3 and 4)[2] by Kaser[3] and Koschaker[4] is

8. 2. 31; 8. 4. 16; though I certainly do not say that litigation on the points involved in these particular texts would have been centumviral.

[1] Op. cit. 106 n. 69.

[2] Koschaker and Kaser attach importance to the occurrence of the word *iudex* in several places in these two titles (*de hereditatis petitione* and *si pars hereditatis petatur*). But these titles contain no excerpts from jurists earlier than Neratius and Celsus, and, quite apart from the question of possible interpolation, can scarcely be called in evidence on this point for the Republic or the first century of the Empire. There is no difficulty in conceding that a formulary *hereditatis petitio* with an *unus iudex* existed later, in the classical period.

[3] Op. cit. 39 n. 24.

[4] Op. cit. 686.

D. 40. 7. 29. 1, which concerns *hereditatis petitio* and speaks of a party losing his case through *iniuria iudicis*. If the phrase *iniuria iudicis* were found only here in the Digest, there might be some force in the text as showing that a single judge heard the case; but in fact *iniuria iudicis* occurs fairly frequently[1] and seems to be no more than a compendious expression for 'judicial wrongdoing'. No more can be got out of the text than the idea that the party has been defeated through the wrongdoing of *a* judge, not of *the* judge. I can see no reason, for instance, why the very case envisaged here might not have been the kind of case in which the drunken judges in Macrobius[2] were involved, if one of them through malice or frivolity persuaded his colleagues to make a short end to the case, however unjustly, in order to resume the binge.

As for the question whether there was a 'floor' to the centumviral jurisdiction, there is no doubt a predisposition to presume such a thing from the rationalistic idea that a weighty and numerous board of judges could scarcely concern itself with bagatelles or those who litigated over them (the *nugatores* of the Macrobius passage just mentioned).[3] The hard evidence for the existence of any such 'floor' is, however, not very impressive; it is said by Kaser[4] to be found in Paul. *Sent.* 5. 9. 1:

Substitutus heres ab instituto, qui sub condicione scriptus est, utiliter sibi institutum hac stipulatione cavere compellit, ne petita bonorum possessione res hereditarias deminuat; hoc enim casu ex die interpositae stipulationis duplos fructus praestare compellitur. Huius enim praeiudicium a superiore differt, quo quaeritur an ea res de qua agitur maior sit centum sestertiis; ideoque in longiorem diem concipitur.

[1] e.g. D. 3. 3. 46. 4, 15. 1. 50. pr., 17. 2. 52. 18, 20. 5. 12. 1, 40. 7. 29. 1, 46. 1. 67, 46. 8. 22. 4.

[2] *Saturn.* 3. 16. 15.

[3] Kaser, *RZPrR* 39 n. 24, says simply that disputes about trivial inheritances would hardly have been brought before 'the great court'. Apart from Pliny's testimony (see p. 35 n. 4 below), there is the strong possibility that, if in a big case all the divisions or chambers of the court sat together, in a small case the issue might have been tried by a single such division. We do not know how big such centumviral divisions may have been; the conferring of the centumviral presidency on *decemviri* suggests the possibility of relatively small divisions of about ten judges.

[4] Op. cit. 39 n. 24.

This is supposed to be a hint that the *centumviri* heard cases only where the value of the inheritance was not less than 100,000 sesterces. Relevance to the centumviral jurisdiction is denied this passage altogether by Bozza,[1] but Kaser,[2] following Lenel,[3] sees in the procedure a method of determining before which jurisdiction eventual litigation would come (if the value were less than 100,000 sesterces, it would be the *unus iudex*). Wlassak objected[4] to this interpretation when it was first put forward by Lenel, on the very sensible ground that it implied that parties who might not have the slightest intention of ever litigating would be forced into this cumbersome procedure of valuation in order to fix the seat of jurisdiction in the event of litigation in fact occurring; and he drew attention also, quite properly, to the passage in Pliny's letters[5] where he complains of being taken up with *centumvirales causae* of no substance (*parvae et exiles*). To this I would add two further considerations (though by the date of the *Pauli Sententiae* the issue is of no importance to the present purpose anyway): firstly, that any such rule could not have applied in the pre-money economy of the early Republic when, as explained above, I believe the *centumviri* already existed; and secondly, that such a rule would make no sense in any case in which the exercise of *patria potestas* depended on the outcome of an inheritance trial.[6] How could the value of the paternal authority be computed in money?

I summarize my conclusions so far about the *centumviri* as follows: it was a court of archaic date, of a deliberately representative composition, and with a jurisdiction in inheritance cases both great and small. There remains the central question of why such a thing as the centumviral jurisdiction should be found in coexistence with the *unus iudex*.

In order to see the size of this problem, it is necessary to put aside the distracting feature of the *recuperatores* (a special case arising in special circumstances, as I hope to show) and to concentrate on the extraordinary contrast between a very large public court, on the one hand, and a *iudicium privatum* conducted

[1] Op. cit. 90–1. [2] Loc. cit. [3] *Edictum perpetuum*, 515 ff.
[4] *Römische Prozessgesetze*, i. 227 ff. [5] 2. 14. 1. [6] See below, pp. 32 ff.

by a single judge, possibly under the roof of his own house,[1] on the other; each kind of jurisdiction handling matters which would, in our eyes, be equally parts of the civil or private law. Very few explanations of this contrast have so far been forthcoming. It cannot lie in the high material value of the property in dispute (assuming, for the sake of argument, that Kaser is right in thinking the *centumviri* operated only above the level of 100,000 sesterces), because no analogous provision existed for the adjudication of cases in contract or delict where the material value of the case might just as easily be very large, but where the jurisdiction of the *unus iudex* (unless 'recuperatorial' conditions existed)[2] was apparently exclusive. An explanation offered by Marrone[3] is that no tribunal with lesser prestige than the *centumviri* could have effected such invasions of the private sphere as, for example, the development of the notion of the *inofficiosum testamentum*, which involved passing judgment on the intimate affairs of a private individual and on his family relations. This was undoubtedly a big inroad on private discretion. But is it clear that the *centumviri* invented it as distinct from administering it? And surely it was no more startling as a piece of law reform than many innovations of the praetor in the same area, such as the edicts *unde cognati* and *unde vir et uxor*. In any case, Marrone's view will not account for the origination and retention of the *centumviri* up to the time when the *querela* developed;[4] it can hardly be supposed that at a remote period such a development was actually foreseen and facilitated by the creation of an unusually prestigious court.

Kunkel[5] saw in the *centumviri* an extremely archaic judicial organ which may originally have had a criminal jurisdiction, with (as has been said above) a numerous composition in order to spread the odium of its judgments widely and so reduce the chances of vendetta; in comparison with which the figure of the *unus iudex*, so far from being central and primeval in Roman legal history, is a later and secondary phenomenon. Without

[1] See below, pp. 103 ff. [2] See below, pp. 47 ff. [3] Op. cit. 42–3.

[4] Its date is not certain, but is placed by some as late as the end of the Republic; e.g. von Woess, *Das römische Erbrecht und die Erbanwärter*, 200 ff.

[5] Op. cit. 115 ff.

attempting a critique of Kunkel's theory,[1] it can be said that, even allowing it to be correct, it still would not explain why, once the *unus iudex* had appeared, he should have been kept out of the field of inheritance cases and why these should have been reserved to the *centumviri*.

Another line of opinion, of which Behrends[2] may serve as a representative, sees in the *centumviri* the results of a democratizing movement aimed at abridging the senatorial monopoly in the courts. On this view, which of course entails giving the *centumviri* a later date than I think justifiable (as I have explained above), the main purpose of the reform was to give urban artisans and the smaller landowners courts for dealing with their most important litigation (inheritance and, according to Behrends, status cases), on which the classes to which they belonged would have a numerical majority. Apart from the difficulty of reconciling this view with the 'prestige' image of the *centumviri* (to say nothing of any restriction of centumviral jurisdiction to cases *above* a certain value), I cannot see why a semi-political reform like this should have arbitrarily stopped at inheritance (or status) cases. It is easy to say these were the 'most important' kinds of case, but if the legislative reformer posited by Behrends had got this far, why might he not have gone on to throw into the lap of the *centumviri* other litigation as well—*vindicationes*, actions in contract and delict—which might be just as serious, and just as sensitive to the operation of an unsympathetic senatorial judiciary, as the loss of an inheritance?

It seems to me that there is some much more vital factor at work in the history of the *centumviri;* a factor perhaps buried, or no longer so obvious, by the end of the Republic, but the uncovering of which is crucial to elucidating the Roman Republican judicature.

It can be admitted at once that the surviving sources bearing directly on the *centumviri*, though numerous enough, do not provide the answer to this problem, and what I propose is no more than a hypothesis—a *ratio* for the existence of a well-defined

[1] The 'averting-vendetta' part of the theory is without support in the texts.

[2] Op. cit. 106.

centumviral jurisdiction side by side with that of the *unus iudex*—which at least is not contradicted by the sources, and which disposes of the problems presented by one or two conspicuous peculiarities of the centumviral court. This *ratio*, in my submission, is to be found, not in any movement of political reform, nor in the supposed advantages of a court strong in numbers or in prestige, but in the area of the court's operation. We might look, then, at the law of inheritance, to see if it contains any feature of consequence, absent from, say, the law of obligations or other litigious material, which offers a clue. In doing so, the obvious way to begin is to look at the sequence of descent of an inheritance, because this is the point at which conflicting interests can emerge.

Here at once we meet a feature unfamiliar in modern law and with very few[1] parallels in Roman law itself: namely that in the descent of the estate of an intestate (intestate either because no will was ever made, or because a will is declared void) the old Roman law[2] gave the inheritance first to the *sui heredes*—i.e. to those who on the death of the *de cuius* became *sui iuris*; next, in default of these, to the *proximi adgnati*—a concept narrowly interpreted[3]—but in default of both *sui heredes* and *proximi adgnati*, to the members of the *gens* of which the deceased was a member; and it will be recalled that, early in the litany of topics given by Cicero as typical centumviral material, we find *gentilitates*.[4]

The nature of the Roman *gens* and the part it played in the early history of the Roman state has been very fully discussed. It was a group based on a blood relationship, real or presumed because of identity of name, and as such was in the same generic category as *curia* and *tribus*, as originally understood. The *gens* bore some relationship to the *curia*,[5] probably by way of the

[1] *Tutela, cura*: *Laudatio Turiae*, 13 ff.; XII Tab. 7a; *Rhet. ad Her.* 1. 13. 23; Cic. *Tusc.* 3. 5. 11.

[2] i.e. before the introduction of praetorian reforms.

[3] Gaius, *Inst.* 3. 12: *nec in eo iure successio est. ideoque, si agnatus proximus hereditatem omiserit vel, antequam adierit, decesserit, sequentibus nihil iuris ex lege competit.*

[4] *De orat.* 1. 173; see also 1. 176; p. 24 n. 1.

[5] Jolowicz, *Historical Introduction to Roman Law* (2nd edn. by Barry Nicholas), 18.

*curia* being composed of a certain number of *gentes*.[1] The *curiae* in their turn were distributed among the original three *tribus* (Ramnes, Tities, Luceres); according to tradition,[2] each of these three tribes contained ten *curiae*. But even when the purely kinship-based *tribus* became rather a local political division, the new *tribus* must still have contained a very strong element of kinship, and the disappearance of all connection between *curia* and *tribus* seems most unlikely.[3] Accordingly, the triple nexus *gens-curia-tribus* must have survived, though in what precise form or degree of strength it is now impossible to determine.

This observation is uncertain, and obscure in detail; but it seems to me a very striking feature of the *centumviri* that, in the very field where the *gens* had, right into the late Republic and even the early Empire, a contingent interest in the descent of an inheritance, the court before which inheritance cases are litigated is one constituted—on the evidence of our only authority—on a system at once representative and in which the representation is based, so to speak, on 'constituencies' not entirely dissociated from the *gens*.

[1] Kaser, *RPR* 67.

[2] Cic. *De repub*. 2. 14; Livy 1. 13. 6; Dion. Hal. 2. 7; Plut. *Rom*. 14; D. 1. 2. 2. 2 (Pomponius); Festus L. 42.

[3] It is, firstly, improbable that if the 'Servian' system had been a genuine radical reform, whereby the organization of the people was changed from a structure based on kinship to one based on locality, irrespective of kinship, the word *tribus* would have been arbitrarily kept in use to mean something quite different from its sense in the immediately preceding period. It is as though a modern reform were to abandon some traditional system of local government electoral units such as 'wards', but retain the same word 'wards' to mean some entirely different electoral unit, e.g. based on income bracket, if such a thing could be imagined. Secondly, the survival of the family element as predominant even in the new locality-based tribes is evidenced by the fact that the fifteen original rural *tribus*, excluding the *Claudia*, all bear the names of *gentes*: see L. R. Taylor, *Voting Districts of the Roman Republic*, 6–7. See also Kubitschek, *RE* 6a. 2493 (s.v. *tribus*), quoting with approval Schulze, *Geschichte lateinischer Eigennamen*, 545, whose study of the political organization disclosed by the Iguvian tablets showed a local, not a gentilician structure, but one resting upon, or connected with, a gentilician system. Moreover, there is nothing surprising, in an agrarian community, in a strongly marked kinship element among most or all of the inhabitants of a particular locality. In Ireland, and no doubt other places, there are very many instances of district-names which are not just *derived* from the names of families or clans, but are actually identical in form with family or tribal names: e.g. Uí Maine, Uíbh Eachach, Uíbh Laoghaire, Síol mBroin, Clann Aodha Buí, Clann Mhuiris.

Festus is reported by Paulus Diaconus as writing:

Centumviralia iudicia a centumviris sunt dicta. Nam cum essent Romae triginta et quinque tribus, quae et curiae sunt dictae, terni ex singulis tribubus sunt electi ad iudicandum, qui centumviri appellati sunt, et, licet quinque amplius quam centum fuerint, tamen, quo facilius nominarentur, centumviri sunt dicti.

On this passage it must firstly be observed, and with emphasis, that it is our *only* purported source of information on the mode of composition of the *centumviri*. It seems to me that two approaches to it are possible.

We can, firstly, take Festus at his apparent word in regard to the *tribus* being the 'constituencies' from which the court was selected. This, if related simply to the final structure of the *tribus*—i.e. as from 241 B.C.—whereby the more recently created of the 35 *tribus* were denominated not by a family name but by that of a place,[1] and whereby accordingly the actual basis of election of *centumviri* would no longer have been purely or even largely a representation of the people organized according to blood, would not sustain the idea here advanced, namely that the very important gentilician rights in succession account for the familial basis of the centumviral court. But of course there is no need to maintain, alongside this hypothesis, the further proposition that the centumviral court, once established, was always, and with perfect consistency, so composed; for my purpose it is enough to suggest the original sense of this court, and since, as I have tried to argue above, the court belongs to the very oldest stratum of Roman legal history, long before the *tribus* could be said to have lost all trace of internal kinship—which certainly cannot have happened as an immediate result of the 'Servian' reform—the possibility remains perfectly open that the *centumviri* were drawn from the *tribus* for the *original* reason (however subsequently diluted in practice) that a court so formed would necessarily cover a wide spread of *gentes*.

However, another, somewhat more radical approach to the Festus text is possible. It will be noticed that what he says is

[1] L. R. Taylor, loc. cit.

*cum essent Romae triginta et quinque tribus, quae et curiae sunt dictae,* etc. This is not the only passage in ancient literature which appears to equate or to confuse *tribus* and *curiae* with each other,[1] though it is not possible to contend that they were ever treated as identical in reality. But on the face of the Festus text, the following possibility must exist: that Festus, or possibly Paulus who quotes him, used *tribus* in an explanatory way, as being perhaps a more familiar expression to his readers, but added that the particular kind of 'tribe' he meant in this context was actually called a *curia.* If then what we are really being told is that the centumviral court was recruited, not from the *tribus* in the strict sense, but from the *curiae*—and I must emphasize again that since this passage is our only source of any kind on the court's composition, its interpretation is absolutely crucial—then the 'familial' base of the centumviral jurisdiction, and simultaneously its connection with the *gentes* (and with the *comitia calata*: see below) comes much more sharply into view than if one is left with the *tribus* only.

In view of the fact that Festus himself lived long after the creation of the centumviral court (on any theory as to its date), and of the fact that Paulus Diaconus, who lived in the eighth century, may have tampered with the Festus original, the passage does not lend itself to any kind of certainty; in addition, there is the problem with the second interpretation here suggested, that it posits a number of 35 *curiae,* which is unsupported elsewhere in Roman literature—except for another passage from Festus/Paulus[2]—and thus produces an uneasy numerical coincidence between the well-established 35 *tribus* and the virtually unestablished 35 *curiae.* At the same time, it would be wrong to dismiss the possibility, to which Festus lends at least some colour, that the original 'constituencies' for the centumviral court were not in fact the *tribus,* as he has been generally understood to say, but the *curiae.*

Whichever (if either) of the two hypotheses advanced above

[1] See Kübler, *RE* 4. 1818–19 (s.v. *curia*), who lists the few late sources on the matter, but makes short work of any suggestion that the *curiae* might ever have numbered 35, or had anything like identity with the *tribus.*

[2] L. 42 s.v. *curia.*

is preferred, it seems to me that a familial base for the *centumviri* is extremely probable, at any rate so far as the primeval *centumviri* are concerned, and that this base corresponds with the strongly familial setting of the law of inheritance most particularly where the contingent rights of the *gentiles* are concerned. A court so composed was inherently capable of containing the representatives of a group, or groups[1] of persons, with a direct potential interest in the devolution of a deceased's estate, accompanied, however, by a very large majority of representatives of 'neutral' *gentes*.

Some further remarks may be appropriate here on the subject of what might be called the legitimacy, in Roman eyes, of the affairs of one family being submitted to the scrutiny of a large range of other families.

The most striking instance of this is the role of the *comitia calata* (a special designation, in this setting, of the *comitia curiata*) in the making of wills and the carrying out of adrogations. What is the reason for the peculiar publicity attached to the comitial testament? Note that an outright transfer of a man's whole property might have been made *inter vivos*, in the earliest times of which we have knowledge, with far less publicity: *res mancipi* could be effectively conveyed with as few as six witnesses (of whom all, so far as the law apparently went,[2] might have been members of a single family; they might all have been adult brothers of the purchaser), while *res nec mancipi* could be transferred without witnesses at all. But in order to effect a transfer which would operate after death, the representatives of the people, *organized according to kin-groupings*, had to accord permission.

A similar problem arises with adrogation. Why was *adoptio*, i.e. the transfer of a person from one *patria potestas* to another, possible without more publicity than *mancipatio* attracted, while

[1] In one centumviral case of which Cicero speaks (*De orat*. I. 176) the issue was the conflicting interests not of two individuals but of two *gentes*: *Quid? qua de re inter Marcellos et Claudios patricios centumviri iudicarunt, cum Marcelli ab liberti filio stirpe, Claudii patricii eiusdem hominis hereditatem gente ad se rediisse dicerent; nonne in ea causa fuit oratoribus de toto stirpis ac gentilitatis iure dicendum?*

[2] Gaius, *Inst*. I. 119, says simply *adhibitis non minus quam quinque testibus civibus Romanis puberibus, et praeterea alio eiusdem condicionis qui libram aeneam teneat*.

*adrogatio*—the subordination of a person *sui iuris* to another's *patria potestas*—again required the authorization of the people organized in a system of family representation?

The Roman sources give no direct answers to these questions, but the suggestion is strong, in the simple facts known to us, that the survival or extinction of a family and its *sacra*, or its material prosperity, was something which in the original Roman state seemed of public importance, and upon which other families, so to speak, kept an eye. As Kaser[1] says, despite the 'witness' element in the etymology of *testamentum*, it can hardly be the case that the *comitia calata* had no function but that of 'witnessing' the designation of an heir; some element of authorization must have been present; and the same must go for *adrogatio*, which—in so far as distinct in form if not in purpose from the nomination of an heir[2]—involved the extinction of the family cult of the person *sui iuris* who had been adrogated. It is hard to present an analogue from the individualistic modern world which might illustrate this interest of all other families in the affairs of one or two families; perhaps the nearest, though no doubt facile parallels are to be found in public international law and practice, whereby disorder or suffering in one country, or a dispute between two, can attract the organized attention of all other civilized states.

Accordingly, I am inclined to see the key to the centumviral jurisdiction in inheritance cases in the residual right of the *gentiles* to inherit upon the failure of *sui heredes* or *proximi adgnati* on intestacy. (Exactly how the rights of the *gentiles* were enjoyed in practice is a mystery; but it is perfectly clear that the *ius gentilicium* in succession was in full operation up to and beyond the end of the Republic.[3]) In such a case the party that stands to gain is one of the families making up the collection of family units organized in *tribus* and *curiae*, and the function of the centumviral court, with its peculiar family-based composition, is—as with adrogation and comitial wills—to keep a watch on the

[1] *RPR* 105. [2] Kaser, *RZPrR* 67.

[3] See the evidence of Cic. *De orat.* 1. 176; *Verr.* 2. 1. 115; Catullus, 68. 119 ff.; Suetonius, *Divus Julius* 1. 2; Watson, *Succession*, 180–1.

*gens* in question, whether to ensure that its members get their lawful due, or to ensure that they do not get what is not due to them. As with all arbitration not squarely based on institutionalized *officium iudicis*, the psychological motive is to preserve a balance in which an element of understanding and of unconcern (most of the families standing neither to lose nor to gain) acts as a check on the elements of interest and partiality (the families which will be richer or poorer depending on the outcome of the case).[1]

If this conception of the *ratio* behind the centumviral jurisdiction can be tentatively accepted, it is worth going back to the *ius gentilicium*, the rights of the *gentiles*, to see whether any other part of these rights may have been similarly treated in the context of litigation. Apart from rights of inheritance, the *gentiles* were entitled to the statutory wardship (*tutela legitima*) of *impuberes* and of women *sui iuris*,[2] and also to the care of *furiosi* and *prodigi*.[3] The actions based on the relationships of *cura* and *tutela* were, in historical times, respectively the *actio negotiorum gestorum* and the *actio tutelae*;[4] both were *bonae*

[1] Professor Kaser has privately expressed his disbelief in the idea that the representatives of, say, 98 *gentes* would have any real interest in the contingent gain or loss of an inheritance by one or two others. Apart from the common interest in the individual family evidenced by the involvement of the *comitia calata* in adrogation—what Heuss, *Römische Geschichte* (2nd edn.), 15, calls a 'soziale Aushilfsleistung'—there are surely analogues elsewhere in legal history. In the modern world the English idea of 'trial by one's peers' comes to mind; as also does the practice whereby the International Court of Justice normally contains a judge from each of the contending states, as well as a majority of 'neutral' judges. As for the infrequency of cases in which the interest of a *gens* would be involved—which Professor Kaser also mentions—while the possible immediate succession of the *gentiles* on the failure of a closer heir might, in any given hundred cases, be rare enough, the passage of a *hereditas* from a member of one *gens* to a member of another—with the consequent instant emergence of a future contingency in favour of the latter—must have been very common.

J. A. Crook comments further: if it was so crucial to have the *centumviri* adjudicate matters vital to the *gentes*, why did they not adjudicate other such matters as well e.g. the *actio familiae erciscundae*? My reply would be that in the *actio familiae erciscundae* the persons who stand to gain or lose through the adjudication are all known beforehand, i.e. the heirs who seek by arbitration a peaceful division of their common property, and who, as Kaser puts it (*RZPrR* 42), make no contradictory assertions against one another. A contingent right of the *gentiles* is not part of the picture at all.

[2] Kaser, *RPR* 54.

[3] Kaser, *RZPrR* 67.

[4] Kaser, *RPR* 587, 365.

*fidei iudicia* and thus, at whatever stage the *bonae fidei* formula was applied to situations arising from *tutela* and *cura*, they necessarily belonged to the sphere of the *unus iudex*; but there is nothing to exclude the possibility—which I admit is completely without foundation in the surviving sources—that, before the rise of the *bonae fidei iudicia*, disputes arising from *tutela* and *cura*, with their close relevance to family property and the potential involvement of the *gens*, came before the *centumviri*. This possibility would of course in its turn require an explanation of how the centumviral jurisdiction came to lose *tutela* and *cura* while retaining inheritance matters; one simple answer would be that the *bonae fidei* formula offered a flexible mode of judging the quality of guardianship, while in litigation about whether X was or was not entitled to inheritance, or whether he had or had not been wrongfully excluded from benefit under a will, the *bona fides* of either party to the case could scarcely become material to the issue.

If we turn now to a very striking attribute of the *centumviri*, it may be that it will harmonize better with the views expressed above as to the *ratio* and jurisdiction of that court than with any other theory so far advanced. This is the procedural peculiarity adverted to by Gaius, *Inst.* 4. 30–1, when he briefly accounts for the transition from *legis actio* to *formula* as being a reaction against the excessive technicality associated with the former:

Itaque per legem Aebutiam et duas Iulias sublatae sunt istae legis actiones, effectumque est ut per concepta verba, id est per formulas, litigaremus. Tantum ex duabus causis permissum est lege agere: damni infecti et si centumvirale iudicium futurum est. Sane quidem, cum ad centumviros itur, ante lege agitur sacramento apud praetorem urbanum vel peregrinum. Damni vero infecti nemo vult lege agere, sed potius stipulatione quae in edicto proposita est obligat adversarium suum, idque et commodius ius et plenius est. Per pignoris . . .

Why, in such a fundamental procedural revolution as the replacement of *legis actio* by *formula*, should just these two[1] kinds

[1] Aulus Gellius, *N.A.* 16. 10. 8; mentions only one survival (*nisi in legis actionibus centumviralium causarum*), saying nothing about *damnum infectum*.

of case have been left behind? What prevented centumviral cases, or cases about *damnum infectum*, from being clothed in a *formula* like all other cases?

The explanations offered for this—when the problem attracts attention at all—are very feeble. Lévy-Bruhl,[1] followed by Watson,[2] thought the survival of the *legis actio* for centumviral cases is easily understood as being merely the retention of a 'venerable' procedural form for such a prestigious tribunal which handled matters of such admitted importance as succession cases. But surely the very importance of such cases would have given them, above all others, a claim upon the benefits of an improved procedure, in which the gain or loss of an inheritance would no longer depend on the *nimia subtilitas* which had attracted such general unpopularity (*odium*)? With regard to *damnum infectum*, Lévy-Bruhl[3] thought the question of why an exception was made here less easy to answer, and concluded that the nature of *damnum infectum* required perhaps immediate and direct interference by the party threatened, and that, assuming the *legis actio* in question was *pignoris capio*, this direct remedy survived as the best-adapted to meet emergencies 'until the praetor had created a more effective and modern remedy'. But by the time of the *leges Iuliae*, and indeed long before them, the edictal machinery was virtually complete,[4] and Lévy-Bruhl's idea requires us to suppose that the *cautio damni infecti*—the effective and modern praetorian remedy—was not invented until after the *leges Iuliae*. This is certainly wrong; Watson[5] points to texts[6] which establish its existence in 58 B.C. and possibly even as early as 73 B.C. However, Watson's own explanation[7] for the exceptional survival of the *legis actio* in *damnum infectum* is that it must be 'due to chance', and the *legis actio* used in *damnum infectum* cases (he believes *pignoris capio*) was simply 'overlooked' by

[1] *Recherches sur les actions de la loi*, 325 ff.

[2] *Property*, 128.

[3] Op. cit. 326 ff.

[4] Kelly, 'The Growth-Pattern of the Praetor's Edict', 1 *Irish Jurist* (1966) 341 ff.

[5] *Succession*, 139 ff.

[6] Pliny *N.H.* 36. 2. 5, 6; Cic. *Verr.* 2. 1. 146.

[7] Loc. cit.

the reforming legislation; omitted inadvertently, as one might say of a modern enactment, from the schedule of repeals. This will not do.

It seems to me a sound approach to this problem to look for some factor inherent in *legis actio* procedure, but essentially absent from the formulary procedure—or vice versa—which would, because of the practical nature of the two cases excepted, outweigh whatever value the Aebutian/Julian reforms might have had in those cases. Here I think that something like the right answer has been found, so far as *damnum infectum* is concerned, by Mozzillo,[1] who saw that the contingent nature of the plaintiff's grievance did not fit into the structure of an ordinary *formula* with its *condemnatio/absolutio*, above all in view of the exclusively pecuniary *condemnatio* common to all formulary actions.[2] 'In reality', Mozzillo wrote, 'there would have been nothing to prevent the reformer from changing the ancient civil law action into an *agere per formulas*, but the only possible judgment would then have been for *quanti ea res erit*, difficult if not impossible to determine exactly, since the damage was still only apprehended.'

There is, however, a further consideration, neglected by Mozzillo, arising from the *condemnatio pecuniaria* of the formulary system, namely, that by contrast with this procedure, the *legis actio* permitted what might effectively amount to a judgment *in rem ipsam* (in the sense meant by Gaius),[3] whether the *legis actio* used in *damnum infectum* was *pignoris capio* or was *sacramento* or *per iudicis arbitrive postulationem*.[4] This would seem a very solid reason, grounded in the nature of the complaint itself, for keeping *damnum infectum* out of the formulary system and within a system, in other respects archaic and excessively

[1] *Contributi allo studio delle stipulationes praetoriae*, 123 n. 133.

[2] Gaius, *Inst.* 4. 48: *omnium autem formularum quae condemnationem habent ad pecuniariam aestimationem condemnatio concepta est.*

[3] *Inst.* 4. 48 continues: *itaque, et si corpus aliquod petamus, veluti fundum, hominem, vestem, aurum, argentum, iudex non ipsam rem condemnat eum cum quo actum est, sicut olim fieri solebat, (sed) aestimata re pecuniam eum condemnat.* See Kaser, *RZPrR*, 287.

[4] Opinions differ on this point. Lévy-Bruhl (op. cit. 319) and Watson, *Property* 131) favour *pignoris capio*; Mozzillo (op. cit. 83 ff.) favours *iudicis arbitrive postulatio*; Kaser (op. cit. 25 n. 13) favours *sacramentum in personam.*

technical, which might oblige the defendant to submit to direct activity by the plaintiff to abate the conditions which threatened him with damage. Exactly the same kind of considerations underlie the coexistence, in the modern common law, of an award of damages with the granting of a 'quia timet' injunction commanding the defendant to make safe a situation from which the plaintiff apprehends injury.

Now if the explanation of one of the exceptions listed by Gaius is to be found in the *condemnatio pecuniaria* of the formulary system, it would be reasonable to explore the hypothesis that much the same, if not exactly the same reason is behind the survival of *legis actio* procedure in centumviral cases.

As has been seen, centumviral cases were inheritance cases. If we look closely at what this implies, reasons instantly spring into view which make it a highly attractive notion that the *centumviri* judged an issue raised by *legis actio* rather than *per formulas*, not because of the 'venerable' nature of the former procedure, but because the nature of the procedure did not constrain them to pronounce a judgment in purely money terms. This would mean that a plaintiff raising *hereditatis petitio* by means of *legis actio sacramento* would not, if he succeeded in having his *sacramentum* declared *iustum*, be obliged to content himself with a money assessment of what the court had declared to be rightfully his, but would be within the law if he actually took possession of the property which was the substance of the inheritance; if this involved force which injured the defendant or damaged his property, no action could lie against the heir now judicially so declared; since his *sacramentum* was *iustum*, he would not have been guilty of *iniuria* in either the Aquilian or the praetorian sense.

In support of this hypothesis, I would like to advance some considerations which seem to me collectively quite powerful. There is, firstly, the strictly legal question of the position of someone judicially recognized as heir in consequence of an action brought to establish his status as such. If he has instituted a *legis actio sacramento*, he must formally assert his entitlement as heir over some object taken to stand for the whole inheritance,[1] and if his *sacramentum* is then found to be *iustum*, he is surely—and by his own very deliberate act—expressing himself as heir by a mode even more emphatic than *aditio* or *cretio*. At the moment of favourable judgment, therefore, he must have reached the point from which he can no longer recede: the point expressed by the post-Roman maxim *semel heres, semper heres*. Moreover, as well as whatever benefits the inheritance may bring him, there will be liabilities, in particular the burdensome liability—or so it was thought by some[2]—to perpetuate the family *sacra*. If the judgment of the *centumviri* were now commuted into a simple decree for money, representing the commercial value of land, slaves, stock, goods, and chattels, together, in some cases, with a valuation of his familial authority (as would necessarily be the case in the formulary system), the entire corporeal content of his position as heir would have dropped away, leaving nothing but a sum of money along with a liability to perpetuate the family cult, which it is impossible to imagine being commuted into terms of either money credit or money debit, and which could scarcely attach to a defendant who had just been declared *not* to be heir, even though he might hold on to the corporeal components of the *hereditas* by paying the *condemnatio pecuniaria*. Consideration of this absurdity seems to me to afford a very good reason why centumviral, i.e. inheritance, cases were not brought under the formulary procedure, and why the *legis actio* was perpetuated in such cases, where what a successful plaintiff is primarily aiming at is to take the actual inheritance into his hands as a whole.

A second, certainly related consideration is the *unique* character of the typical inheritance. It will be recalled that the modern remedy of specific performance of a contract of sale is limited to cases in which the plaintiff has been disappointed of receiving something of its nature unique, such that damages for breach alone would be an insufficient remedy. This regularly

[1] Gaius, *Inst.* 4. 16.

[2] Note the byword for a piece of good fortune without snags, *hereditas sine sacris*: Plautus *Capt.* 775, *Trin.* 484; see Watson, *Succession*, 5–6.

means, in Irish law, that a contract for the sale of land may be specifically enforced by the purchaser, as the courts take the view that any piece of land is essentially unique; the same would hold of a painting or a manuscript, though not of an industrial artefact whose duplicate, or something like it, could be bought out of an award of damages for failure to deliver the one actually contracted for.[1] It may be imagined with how much greater power the notion of justice which sustains the modern specific performance would operate against a mere money compensation system where the objects in issue—the corporeal components of the inheritance—comprise not only chattels of no peculiar value, but also land and buildings which may be the object of considerable intangible value through long-standing family association, and above all, human beings—the slave *familia*—with whom close emotional ties, and certainly also often blood ties may exist.

If we take a passage like Paulus, D. 9. 2. 33. pr., this idea may seem persuasive:

> Si servum meum occidisti, non affectiones aestimandas esse puto, veluti si filium tuum naturalem quis occiderit quem tu magno emptum velles, sed quanti omnibus valeret. Sextus quoque Pedius ait pretia rerum non ex affectione nec utilitate singulorum, sed communiter fungi; itaque eum, qui filium naturalem possidet, non eo locupletiorem esse, quod eum plurimo, si alius possideret, redempturus fuit . . .

Note that in both propositions what is envisaged is a child of slave status belonging to his own natural father as his *paterfamilias*, and consequently, in what was no doubt the commonest case, the offspring of an *ancilla* belonging to the father. Here we see—and it is by no means the only instance in the Digest or in Roman literature generally[2]—the human reality behind the presence of *ancillae* in the household: the possibility, if not indeed the likelihood, that unfree children might be the sons or daughters, or half-brothers or half-sisters of the free children (i.e. the *sui heredes*) or of the *paterfamilias* himself. No issue so

[1] See, e.g., Keeton and Sheridan, *Equity*, 486.
[2] See, e.g., Gellius *N.A.* 2. 23. 8; Papinian, D. 17. 1. 54.

sensitive, so cruel in defeat, could be imagined as that in which the inheritance left on the decease of the *paterfamilias* has to be litigated by a son or a grandson; no issue in which success would be so empty if it produced nothing more than a judgment in *quanti ea res erit.*[1] So far from being anomalous, so far from having anything to do with the mere 'venerability' of the *legis actio* justifying its retention in succession cases, it seems to me an extremely reasonable and, in the technical modern as well as in the ancient sense, equitable exception from the generality of the Aebutian/Julian reforms that centumviral litigation was kept out of the area of the formulary procedure with its generalized *condemnatio pecuniaria.*[2]

A few final words on this point may be said in connection with the bearing of *hereditas* on the devolution of *patria potestas.* The family authority did not itself pass by inheritance,[3] but it

[1] J. A. Crook has privately objected that the very passage just cited—D. 9. 2. 33. pr.—would provide an argument against my case rather than for it; he thinks the rule *affectiones non aestimandas* might suggest that the *condemnatio pecuniaria* was not in fact out of place in assessing the value of an inheritance. I cannot agree: the Aquilian rule must be read solely in its own context; the very fact that it required statement here suggests that in other contexts it did not apply; and its presence here—to which I draw attention merely to illustrate the strength of such affections—permits no conclusions about the operation of *hereditatis petitio*. In modern Irish or English law, for example, while no damages, or only token damages, are recoverable for bereavement alone in an 'Aquilian' setting of negligence, in the field of family or matrimonial law, e.g. in cases involving the custody of children, the courts virtually give primacy to the protection of human relationships, i.e. *affectiones*.

[2] I am not inclined to persist in the theory I put forward in *Roman Litigation*, 69 ff., as to the reasons behind the *condemnatio pecuniaria*, and I acknowledge the justice of the criticisms of Kaser (84 *ZSS* (1967) 513 ff.) and Pugliese (35 *Tijdschrift* (1967) 298 ff.). Professor Kaser has privately commented on my present view of *condemnatio pecuniaria*. He objects to my suggestion that, since it was inherent in the formulary system, it might have been responsible for the retention of the *legis actio* procedure for centumviral cases, on the ground that by the time of Augustus the old *legis actio sacramento in rem* as described by Gaius (4. 31) would have disappeared and the *legis actio* would have been *per sponsionem praeiudicialem*, implying therefore a later assessment procedure amounting in effect to something like a *condemnatio pecuniaria* subject to a *clausula arbitraria*. But I do not know that there is firm evidence that the *l.a. sacramento in rem* had disappeared by the time of Augustus; Gaius 4. 95, which describes the procedure of roughly a century and a half later, is hardly such evidence. And if one is driven to suppose that a centumviral judgment on a *hereditatis petitio* or *querela* ended in a money assessment even in the time of Augustus, the retention of the *l.a.* procedure really seems an insoluble mystery.

[3] Kaser, *RPR* 98.

is very easy to think of cases which, although overtly about *hereditas*, turn on a question which will equally decide whether one of the parties has or has not paternal authority over the free members of the deceased's family. If X, who appears to be the only free-born son of the deceased and so a *suus heres*, is extruded by Y, who claims not only to be himself entitled as *proximus adgnatus* in default of a *suus heres*, but also that X's failure to deserve the title *suus heres* is due to his being, in fact, unfree, then what X stands to lose is not only the *hereditas* in a purely pecuniary sense, but also his paternal authority over children of his own whom he has begotten in a union which (since it cannot be a *iustum matrimonium* if in fact he is a slave) will, if Y wins, be taken to have engendered children over whom no *patria potestas* can be exercised by X. But if X wins, he will want not only the *hereditas* in the ordinary sense, but the re-establishment of his family relationship as well. If this has been withheld from him by Y (on the grounds perhaps that the children's mother was also unfree, so that her offspring belong to the *hereditas*), the task of quantifying in money the appropriate judgment against Y is clearly very difficult indeed. All the more reason, therefore, not to attempt something which in any case will have no appeal for the successful plaintiff; all the more reason to keep centumviral actions away from the formulary system with its built-in *condemnatio pecuniaria*.

I may conclude this consideration of the centumviral jurisdiction by looking at a question which, while it adds little or nothing to the picture I have tried to present in regard to the reasons for such a jurisdiction, serves nevertheless to adjust our focus on the *centumviri* as an element in the total Roman judicial scene—an element which tends, I think, to be wrongly presented as something marginal, and to be wrongly reduced from its true significance by the constant treatment of the *unus iudex* as the primary and central figure. If an idea can be given of the practical importance of the *centumviri* in litigious life, it will form a useful part of the background against which the figure of the *unus iudex* can be delineated.

There are two ways, it seems to me, of doing this. We can try to estimate the bulk of litigation (relative to the whole) which fell within the centumviral competence; and we can look at what the lay writers let fall in the way of hints as to the relative prominence of the *centumviri* in legal life. The first of these approaches will be postponed until later;[1] the second can be taken now.

Several passages in secular literature from Cicero into the Empire clearly attribute to the *centumviri* a prominence in the life of the courts which is completely at odds with the habitual presentation of them as something subsidiary. Admittedly, some of these texts emphasize the significance of the *centumviri* as a setting for court rhetoric; as will be seen, this was something obviously affected by whether or not court proceedings were in public; centumviral trials were evidently accessible to a numerous audience,[2] so that the passages on centumviral triumphs of oratory, etc., are not to be taken as exactly reflecting the predominance of the centumviral jurisdiction. If they were so taken, the importance of the *unus iudex* would quite unjustifiably shrink to vanishing point.

The Cicero text already cited, *De orat.* 1. 173, envisages three different judicial instances: the praetor (*in iure*), the *unus iudex* (*iudicia privata*), and the *centumviri;* and it is to be noted that the *centumviri* are presented, in this passage, not as an appendix to Cicero's point (the impertinence of junior orators) but as the climax of it. The very same point is made, but with even greater explicitness, a century later by Pliny,[3] when he says that beginners use this court as a training-ground and, much as children learning Greek begin with Homer, these tyro orators start with the court which is the most important one: *nam hic quoque ut illic primum coepit esse quod maximum est.*

As far as practice (as distinct from oratory) goes, Pliny tells us he is 'kept busy' (*distringor*) with centumviral cases (most of them not involving substantial estates,)[4] and calls the centumviral court, in another passage, '*harena mea*' ('my stamping-

[1] Below, pp. 90 ff.

[2] Cic. *Brut.* 197; Pliny *Ep.* 2. 14. 4 ff.; 6. 33. 3; Suet. *rhet.* 30; Martial 6. 38. 5.

[3] *Ep.* 2. 14.

[4] Ibid.; *pleraeque parvae et exiles.*

ground).[1] In different letters[2] he refers to the two occasions, evidently separated by many years, on which he pleaded before the full centumviral court with all four chambers or divisions sitting together; this was clearly very unusual, though we get no hint of the factor justifying this exceptional procedure, mentioned also elsewhere,[3] equally without explanation. In several other passages in his letters Pliny makes bare references to the centumviral jurisdiction, passages not individually assertive, but collectively suggestive of the large importance of the court, despite the circumscribed area of competence which, as we have seen, it possessed.

Tacitus provides further evidence of the central importance of the *centumviri*. In the *Dialogus* 38 he says that nowadays the *causae centumvirales primum obtinent locum*. Formerly, he says, this court was overshadowed by the *splendor aliorum iudiciorum*, so much so that apart from one speech of Asinius Pollio none of the great orators of the earlier generation (he mentions Cicero, Caesar, Brutus, Caelius, and Calvus) had left any oration delivered before the *centumviri*.[4] The point of this passage seems to me to be, not that in those days the *centumviri* were overshadowed by the civil jurisdiction of the *unus iudex* (though it is true that speeches of Cicero survive which were delivered before an *unus iudex* and his *consilium* and before *recuperatores*), but that the criminal jurisdiction of the *quaestiones* was the principal scene simultaneously of rhetoric and of political ambition; surely what Tacitus had in mind, in thinking of Cicero, was his prosecution of Verres or his defence of Milo rather than his speech on behalf of Quinctius or Tullius. If matters had changed by the time of Tacitus, it was because, as he says, *longa temporum quies et continuum populi otium et assidua senatus tranquillitas et maxima principis disciplina ipsam quoque eloquentiam sicut omnia alia pacaverat*; the allusion here seems to

[1] *Ep.* 6. 12. 2.

[2] *Ep.* 1. 18. 3, 4. 24. 1.

[3] Pliny *Ep.* 6. 33. 3; Quint. *Inst. or.* 12. 5. 6; Val. Max. 7. 7. 1.

[4] But Cicero in fact did plead before the *centumviri*; see *De orat.* 2. 98, where he describes his appearance in this court against Curio, who was acting for 'the brothers Cosius', and pays high tribute to the oratory of Curio on this occasion.

include that aspect of the Roman revolution which had transformed, among other things, the criminal jurisdiction by progressively substituting for the old *quaestio*-trials hearings by the princeps himself and by the Senate. It is, as I have admitted, quite clear that comparisons drawn from the perspective of an advocate, with his interest in oratorical fame, cannot accurately reflect the relative practical importance of different courts in point of litigation; at the same time, the fact that Pliny and Tacitus leave the *iudicium privatum* completely unmentioned suggests perhaps not only its relative lack of attraction for the advocate but also that its place in the whole judicial structure was (for reasons that I shall suggest later) deliberately unobtrusive.

Two passages from Suetonius reinforce this notion. One of them is a very short notice of the life of C. Sallustius Crispus Passienus[1] in which it is stated that he 'willingly'[2] undertook many cases before the *centumviri*, for which his statue was later erected in the *basilica Iulia*; the passage is not very illuminating, though again, whatever practice this orator may have had in *iudicia privata* does not seem worth mentioning. The other passage is of much greater interest; it describes how Vespasian went about normalizing life after his victory in the civil struggles of 68–9: *Sorte elegit per quos rapta bello restituerentur quique iudicia centumviralia, quibus peragendis vix suffectura litigatorum videbatur aetas, extra ordinem diiudicarent redigerentque ad brevissimum numerum.*[3] What seems significant here is that the effects of the civil war on civil justice (leaving aside the *rapta bello*)[4] are represented as felt mainly by the centumviral jurisdiction. In fact Suetonius tells us *in the very same passage* that the troubles had affected all litigation: *Litium series ubique maiorem in modum excreverat manentibus antiquis intercapedine iuris dictionis, accedentibus novis ex condicione tumultuque temporum.* A huge backlog had accumulated, no doubt partly through difficulty in arranging hearings, with lesser availability of judges and witnesses; but the only jurisdiction (apart from the recuperatorial problem of *rapta bello*)

[1] Suet. frg. (Roth), p. 290, lines 10 ff. [2] *Sponte.*
[3] *Vesp.* 10. [4] This was the field of *recuperatores*.

in which special measures seemed necessary to Vespasian, or worth mentioning to Suetonius, was that of the *centumviri*. Possibly a special factor here was that inheritance cases had piled up through the extra deaths occasioned by the wars; but even allowing for this, it is again one's impression that *iudicia privata* were not prominent in the main flow of litigation.

A few further passages may finally be cited from writers of the early Empire to strengthen the impression that the centumviral court, so far from being peripheral to the central figure of the *unus iudex*, was in the layman's eye—certainly liable to be dazzled by the public oratory for which it provided the main stage—almost synonymous with civil justice. Statius[1] includes in a series of compliments to Rutilius Gallicus the statement that he had shed glory on the Ausonian (i.e. Roman) toga and lent judicial wisdom to the *centumviri*. The same poet,[2] in a turgid address to Vitorius Marcellus, in practice as an advocate, advises him to take a holiday in the quiet time of the year:

> Certe iam Latiae non miscent iurgia leges,
> et pacem piger annus habet messesque reversae
> dimisere forum, nec iam tibi turba reorum
> vestibulo querulique rogant exire clientes;
> cessat centeni moderatrix iudicis hasta,[3]
> qua tibi sublimiam nunc celeberrima fames
> eminet . . .

In neither of these passages is there any hint that *iudicia privata* played any part in an advocate's life, or that any other form of civil jurisdiction than the centumviral court existed; and the same may be said of further passages from Statius,[4] from Ovid,[5] and from Martial.[6] It will be later suggested[7] that *iudicia privata*, tried by an *unus iudex*, were held in private perhaps as a rule, even if not absolutely invariably, and this feature of them would certainly tend to depress their

[1] *Silv.* 1. 4. 24.
[2] *Silv.* 4. 4. 39 ff.
[3] A clear reference to the *centumviri*.
[4] *Silv.* 4. 9. 16.
[5] *Pont.* 3. 5. 21 ff.
[6] 6. 38. 5, 7. 63. 7, 10. 19(20). 15 (a reference to Pliny's centumviral practice).
[7] Below, pp. 103 ff.

interest for the ambitious advocate; but that they should have reached the point where, from an advocate's point of view, they might scarcely have existed, is a striking and important fact, which will be evaluated in a later chapter.[1]

[1] J. A. Crook has kindly drawn my attention to Juvenal 7. 115 ff. and Martial 6. 19 as instances of advocates orating before a single judge. The former passage merely makes fun of an advocate who nearly bursts himself in haranguing an oafish judge; the latter is very similar in purpose—the defendant's advocate, in a case about the theft of three nanny-goats, drags half of Roman military history into his discourse. Both passages should in fact be listed as further proofs that the court of the *unus iudex* was not seen—by anyone except an advocate ready to make himself ridiculous—as an appropriate setting for oratory in the grand manner. Both advocates here have in fact neglected the advice of Cicero (*Orator* 72): *quam enim indecorum est, de stillicidiis cum apud unum iudicem dicas, amplissimis verbis et locis uti communibus!*

# II

# The Jurisdiction of *Recuperatores*

THE jurisdiction of the *recuperatores*, while not so radically problematical as that of the *centumviri*, is still somewhat unclear both as regards its origin and as regards its relationship to the jurisdiction of the *iudex unus*. The *recuperatores* have been the subject of two modern studies, by Yvonne Bongert[1] and Bruno Schmidlin;[2] and while both are of great worth, they seem to fall short of absolute conviction on these matters, and to do so by reason of not attributing enough weight to certain features of the *recuperatores* of which the sources give testimony, and, on the other hand, by treating as central a feature which in reality is only secondary.

The traditional doctrine—adhered to by Bongert and Schmidlin—is to the effect that officers called *recuperatores* were first appointed in the setting of international disputes in order to settle outstanding claims; and that their field of operation was gradually extended, to the point where it included certain parts of the domestic litigious sphere, though only in cases where the public interest was affected, or public order threatened. (This latter element of the public interest would have been, accordingly, the continuing common factor with the original purely 'international' character of their jurisdiction.) In cases of this kind—the theory runs—*recuperatores* were appointed to try the issue, because their procedure was both speedy and 'tougher' or more direct[3] than the procedure before a *iudex unus*. The theory thus contains three stages: (1) original competence only in international disputes, but displaying already, therefore, the element of 'public interest'; (2) transition

[1] *Recherches sur les récupérateurs*, Varia III (1952), 99–266.

[2] *Rekuperatorenverfahren*.

[3] 'Zielstrebiger und straffer gestaltet': Kaser, *RZPrR* 143.

to, or adoption into, domestic procedure; (3) application in domestic procedure only where the 'public interest' element was present. We may begin by enquiring whether the supposed original connection of *recuperatores* with international settlements can really be proved.

By far the earliest literary references to *recuperatores* are two passages in Plautus.[1] The only conclusion which Schmidlin draws from these references is that the recuperatorial procedure was already a well-known legal element by the end of the third century B.C.; the passages themselves, however, according to Schmidlin, are of no value for tracing the origin of the *recuperatores*, because in neither passage is there a trace of 'international settlements'. Certainly, there is no such trace in either passage; but to brush these sources aside on the ground that they do not belong to the international sphere seems (particularly since they are the very oldest references to the subject) to beg the question we are trying to solve. According to Schmidlin, no significance attaches to the Plautus references because Plautus was merely trying to depict a Greek, i.e. a foreign judicial instance, and therefore to use the word *recuperatores* (with its allegedly international overtones) would evoke that picture most effectively among his audience. This explanation is altogether unsatisfactory, for two reasons. Firstly, if the Romans really did think of *recuperatores* as an international judicial organ, a reference to them in a purely domestic setting (as is the case in these passages), a setting of pure private law, would be actually misleading and incomprehensible. Secondly, the comedies of Plautus, notwithstanding their Greek models and settings, are overflowing with legal references of pure Roman origin; Plautus thought nothing of using *praetor* and *iudex* with reference to Athens; why then should he, on these two occasions, have gone to such clumsy and ineffective pains to summon up the image of 'abroad'?

Accordingly, the general theory which sees the origin of *recuperatores* in international settlements is absolutely devoid of support in two passages which are at least a century earlier

[1] *Rudens* 1282; *Bacchides* 270.

than the next unambiguous reference to them. The latter must therefore be approached with a certain scepticism, and nothing should be read out of it that cannot be reconciled with the earlier references.

The passage on which the general opinion as to the 'international law' origin of the *recuperatores* rests is an explanation of the word *reciperatio* given by Festus,[1] who in his turn relies on a jurist (Gallus Aelius) who cannot be dated with more precision than to the first century B.C.:

Reciperatio est, ut ait Gallus Aelius, cum inter populum et reges nationesque et civitates peregrinas lex convenit, quomodo per reciperatores reddantur res reciperenturque, resque privatas inter se persequantur.

This passage is certainly evidence for the use of the word *reciperatio* in international arbitrations and settlements. But that is not the same as saying that the words of Gallus Aelius are (as generally assumed) intended as an *exhaustive* definition of the words *reciperare* or *recuperator* or even *reciperatio*; and still less can these words be used to ground the conclusion that the recuperatorial procedure had its origin in the international sphere.

At least three objections can be raised against the conventional interpretation of this passage. Firstly, we find Plautus using the word *recuperatores* a good century earlier, and in a pure private-law context, so that the words of Gallus Aelius cannot possibly have been intended to be an exhaustive definition which might simultaneously suggest the origin of the jurisdiction. Secondly, we know that already in the first century B.C.—i.e. in the age of Gallus Aelius himself—*recuperatores* were used in trials of *iniuria*-actions between Roman citizens, so that this alleged definition cannot by any stretch of language or imagination be represented as complete. Thirdly, this 'definition' contains an element of circularity; if one looks closely at it, all it is really saying is that the name *reciperatio*

[1] Paul ex Fest. 276 (Mueller).

is given to proceedings conducted by *recuperatores* on the international level. This latter consideration is, perhaps, particularly important, given that Gallus Aelius was a jurist and not a grammarian; if one reads the passage carefully, one has the impression that Gallus Aelius, in speaking of *reciperatio*, was *presupposing* a knowledge of what *recuperatores* were, and wished merely to indicate that the word *reciperatio* was used also in this special setting, i.e. when *international* settlements and reparations were adjudicated by *recuperatores*; in other words, what we have here is the technical word for a reparations procedure conducted on the international level by a judicial organ of a type already familiar in the domestic setting. Indeed, modern usage might be said to reflect exactly the same kind of specialized application, in international law, of words and phrases not inherently 'international'; thus the English 'reparations' or German 'Wiedergutmachung', or the English 'mixed arbitral tribunals' or German 'gemischte Schiedsgerichte', are turns of speech which without the least difficulty could be built into, or have originated in, a purely domestic system of private law, but which in practice have a special meaning at international level. Looked at from this point of view, the Festus passage seems very far from being sound evidence that judicial officers called *recuperatores* had their origin in international law; and the problem of the origin and essence of their jurisdiction remains to be solved.

However, those who regard the Festus passage as decisive for the theory that the *recuperatores* had an international-law origin muster other passages in support of it, including two passages from Livy which bear on the years 210 and 171 respectively. These passages should be approached with the reservation that Livy may easily have used the word *recuperatores* in a sense comprehensible to his own contemporaries, and that in the actual events of two centuries earlier which he describes, the word was not used at all; in this—extremely possible—case the passages would, of course, lose all significance so far as concerns the origin of the recuperatorial jurisdiction. But the passages may also be examined on the assumption that in fact

Livy was faithfully reproducing the usage of an earlier age, however large such an assumption may seem.

The first[1] of these passages describes a dispute which arose within the army of Scipio Africanus as to whether the first man to have climbed the walls of Carthago Nova—and so earned the *corona muralis*—was a Roman centurion or a *socius navalis*. The dispute became so bitter that it threatened to involve the entire contingents to which the two contestants belonged, and thus to prejudice the discipline of the whole army. Thereupon:

Scipio tris recuperatores cum se daturum pronuntiasset qui cognita causa testibusque auditis iudicarent uter prior in oppidum transcendisset, C. Laelio et M. Sempronio, advocatis partis utriusque, P. Cornelium Caudinum de medio adiecit eosque tris recuperatores considere et causam cognoscere iussit.

Schmidlin[2] associates this passage with the Festus passage on account of the circumstance that a *socius navalis*—i.e. one not a Roman citizen—was a party to the dispute; this element would have justified the appointment of *recuperatores*, thus confirming their 'international' essence. But the fact is that the whole incident took place *within* the Roman army, and not between two recently belligerent national groups, and certainly not in a manner corresponding to Gallus Aelius' description of *reciperatio*. Later in the same passage Laelius is shown as complaining to Scipio about the bitterness of the disagreement; he represents it not as a conflict between groups of different national origins, but purely as a matter of rivalry between two arms of the service:

stare hinc legionarios milites, hinc classicos, per omnis deos paratos iurare magis quae velint quam quae sciant vera esse, et obstringere periurio non solum suumque caput, sed signa militaria et aquilas sacramentaque religionum.

The second passage from Livy[3] deals with the complaints of the Spanish provincials in the year 171 about extortions by Roman officials:

cum et alia indigna quererentur, manifestum autem esset pecunias

[1] 26. 48. 8. [2] Op. cit. 5–6. [3] 43. 2.

captas, L. Canuleio praetori, qui Hispaniam sortitus erat, negotium datum est ut in singulos, a quibus Hispani pecuniam repeterent, quinos recuperatores ex ordine senatorio daret patronosque quos vellet sumendi potestatem faceret.

According to Schmidlin,[1] this account contains the earliest case of *repetundae* and suggests that the transition of the recuperatorial competence from the international to the domestic sphere was by way of *repetundae* proceedings. This assertion is not correct. Livy himself reports earlier complaints from provincials about extortion; once in the year 204, when the inhabitants of Locri were concerned,[2] and once in 187, when it was the Gaulish tribe of Cenomani.[3] The Spanish case may certainly have been the first in which the investigation was entrusted to a special board of *recuperatores*. But where is there any trace of the supposed 'transition' from international to domestic litigation? When Livy reports earlier cases of extortion in which the Senate or the consuls intervened to do justice, and in which there is no mention at all of *recuperatores*, all one can speak of is, at most, a new procedural mechanism, i.e. *recuperatores* are here for the first time being used in order to deal with extortion cases. But for the proposition that *recuperatores* were for the first time in this case *imported* from the international-law sphere this passage affords absolutely no proof at all. As far as it goes, it is equally consistent with their being imported into the field of *repetundae* from any part whatever of the existing domestic judicial structure. The use of *recuperatores* in a matter concerning foreigners does not necessarily reflect anything of the origin of their jurisdiction; it may equally well be accounted for by some feature of recuperatorial jurisdiction which has, up to now, escaped attention.

Summing up the evidence so far, then, one is driven to conclude that the opinion according to which the *recuperatores* originated in international disputes is incorrect. It is true that, superficially regarded, the *recuperatores* appear to have a jurisdiction which comes frequently into play in contexts not purely of domestic Roman civil law; but this circumstance may as

[1] Op. cit. 20 ff. [2] 29. 16–21. [3] 39. 3. 1.

easily be accidental as essential, and, I repeat, the dominant theory is quite inconsistent with just those passages in which the word *recuperatores* first appears.

In saying that the appearance of *recuperatores* in 'international' settings may be accidental rather than essential, we may look, finally, at two other passages from the very author relied on so heavily by Schmidlin—Livy—in order to show that, even though *recuperatores* appear often enough in such settings, they are not invariably found there. (Neither of these passages is adverted to by Schmidlin.) The first passage[1] describes what Livy calls a *turpe iudicium* rendered by the Romans when called on by the people of Ardea and Aricia to decide the ownership of a disputed piece of land in 446 B.C. The Roman tribes, egged on by the octogenarian Scaptius, declared that the land belonged to neither litigant people, but to the Romans themselves. Livy says the consuls tried to dissuade them from this piece of greed, urging them *ne pessimum facinus peiore exemplo admitterent iudices in suam rem litem vertendo*: their argument included the rhetorical question: *quem enim hoc privatae rei iudicem fecisse ut sibi controversiosam adiudicaret rem*? Naturally I admit the figurative sense of *iudex* in this passage, but I think it significant that although the very elements are present in the case which Schmidlin thinks were seminal in the recuperatorial jurisdiction, Livy never mentions the word *recuperator*. The second passage[2] makes the same point even more strongly. It is from Livy's account of war in Epirus in 198 B.C. and peace negotiations with Philip of Macedonia. The Roman consul's demands were, that *praesidia ex civitatibus rex deduceret; iis, quorum agros urbesque populatus esset, redderet res quae copararent; ceterorum aeque arbitrio aestimatio fieret*. Among Philip's rejoinders was *Si quas quererentur belli clades eae civitates, cum quibus bellatum foret, arbitrio quo vellent populorum, cum quibus pax utrisque fuisset, se usurum*. But the consul *nihil ad id quidem arbitro aut iudice opus esse dicere*. Note that what is being discussed is almost word for word the situation mentioned in Festus' note on *reciperatio;* but *recuperatores* are nowhere mentioned.

[1] 3. 71 ff. [2] 32. 10.

If then we discard the dominant theory, how are we to explain the special recuperatorial jurisdiction otherwise? Is there any discoverable element in this jurisdiction which might justify and explain its exercise in several different procedural contexts? And if the *recuperatores* in fact arose not in the international but in the domestic sphere, how is their competence to be distinguished from that of the *centumviri* and the *iudex unus*? The answer to this question may begin to appear dimly if we go back to the Plautus texts mentioned at the outset.

One of these passages,[1] in which the *leno* bewails the fact that an alleged slave-girl has been judicially taken away from him, is perhaps not very informative; only one thing is absolutely clear, namely the total absence of any trace of 'international' jurisdiction. But the other passage[2] offers perhaps a slight hint. It concerns the claiming of a money debt which the debtor had denied was owing; but

> postquam quidem praetor recuperatores dedit,
> damnatus demum, vi coactus reddidit
> ducentum et mille Philippum.

In this passage the close connection *damnatus . . . vi coactus reddidit* is striking. It is perfectly possible that the *damnatio* and the *coactio* are the acts of different persons—indeed, in view of the general Roman system of civil execution one would be inclined to assume at first sight that the *recuperatores* pronounced the condemnation, and that the forcible extraction of the money was carried out by the plaintiff on foot of the judgment in his favour. On the other hand, if one considers the strong relevance of influence and power to Roman litigation,[3] and if one recalls that the plaintiff in this particular case was a foreigner seeking justice in Ephesus from a citizen of that same city—someone, therefore, who would not typically have at his disposal enough power to enforce a judgment[4]—one is forced to consider, even if at first merely as a hypothetical possibility,

[1] *Rudens* 1282.
[2] *Bacchides* 270 ff.
[3] Kelly, *Roman Litigation*, ch. 2.
[4] Cf. Plautus, *Poenulus* 1403 ff.; and Kelly, op. cit. 44 ff.

that not only the *damnatio* but also the *coactio* was the act of the *recuperatores*. The passage is of course in no way necessarily interpreted thus; but it does offer the basis for such a hypothesis, and one which points to a feature of the recuperatorial jurisdiction which would instantly differentiate it from that of the *iudex unus*: namely, the competence to execute as well as to pronounce judgments. This would simultaneously provide an explanation of recuperatorial jurisdiction free from the supposed connection with international disputes, but also provide a scheme into which the appearance of *recuperatores* in international or quasi-international settings can be fitted. Equipped with this hypothesis, some further passages may now be examined.

According to Bongert[1] and Schmidlin,[2] the 'international' character of the recuperatorial jurisdiction, supposedly established in the main by the Festus passage, is confirmed by the *lex Antonia de Termessibus*. This *plebiscitum* of 71 B.C. contains the following clause:

> Quos Thermenses maiores Pisidae leiberos servosve bello Mithridatis ameiserunt, magistratus pr[ove] magistratu, quoia de ea re iuris dictio erit qu[oque] de ea re in ious aditum erit, ita de ea re ious deicunto iudicia recuperationes danto, utei ie[i] eos recuperare possint.

The purpose of this provision was to ensure the recovery, by the Roman allies of Termessos, of the free men and slaves whom they had lost in the Mithridatic war; and this was evidently to be done via the recuperatorial procedure. But the magistrate is required to afford *two* different things: not only judicial decisions about wrongfully withheld free men and slaves (*iudicia*) but also (if necessary) the actual recovery of such persons (*recuperationes*). Expanding the terse Latin phrase, one can understand the magistral authority as being to grant *iudicia*, or (if defendants were not amenable, or were not disposed to respect an adverse judgment) relief by way of *recuperatio*.

[1] Op. cit. 117. [2] Op. cit. 4.

Schmidlin assumes[1] that the word *recuperationes* here means an assessment procedure which would have been preceded by an adjudication on the issue of liability (*iudicia*). But there is no evidence whatever, no clue in literature or etymology, that *recuperationes* can be translated 'assessment of value'.

On the contrary, perhaps this very passage is the one in which the etymology of the word might most appropriately be looked at. The statute itself shows the object of the whole operation: *utei iei eos recuperare possint*, which is unambiguous: 'in order that these (i.e. the Termessians) may *get them back* (i.e. the lost slaves etc.)'. This, after all, is the basic meaning of *recuperare*. The word itself contains no trace of anything specifically judicial; and, while of course it is not denied that *recuperatores* were judges, when one finds judges carrying a title derived from a particular word or notion, it is a fair assumption that this notion reflects the special feature of this class of judge. The word *recuperare* is often found in Roman literature with objects such as *obsides*, *oppidum*, *provinciam*; and it clearly means simply to 'get back' or 'recover'.[2] Accordingly, one must seriously consider the likelihood that the phrase *iudicia recuperationes* really means 'judgments and [enforcements by way of] recoveries'. What use is it, after all, to the *socii* from Termessos if the Romans merely require their magistrate to establish judicial instances about persons who have disappeared during the war, if provision is not also made for the enforcement of the resulting decisions by the power of the state which the magistrate embodies?

If this interpretation of the *lex Antonia de Termessibus* is fair, then the hypothesis according to which the special feature of *recuperatores* lay in their capacity to enforce as well as to pass judgment will look somewhat more plausible. The question

[1] Op. cit. 17.

[2] Professor Kunkel comments privately that the sense of 'recover', 'wiedererlangen', would suggest the context of restoring things lost through capture in war, rather than the context of several later established recuperatorial activities. I agree that the idea of 'getting something back' must be original in the whole institution of the *recuperatores*, but do not see that there is any necessary connection with post-*war* reparations. There were such things as peacetime robbery, and no doubt goods were more frequently lost in this way than through war.

now is, whether this hypothesis is consistent with the other contexts in which *recuperatores* appear.

Probably the earliest group of cases in which we have certain knowledge of the operation of *recuperatores* is that represented by statutory provisions which fixed public fines for their contravention. Not all of these are precisely dated; the oldest is perhaps the *lex Latina tabulae Bantinae* of the late second century B.C.

The first part of this inscription[1] still preserved contains exact provisions concerning exclusion of certain persons from a series of offices of public honour; these include *iudex*, *arbiter*, and *recuperator*. In the next part it is laid down, in the case of an infringement of the law by a magistrate, that any other magistrate is entitled to claim the appropriate penalty on behalf of the *municipium*. The inscription then continues:

> sei postulabit quei petet, p[raetor] recuperatores . . . [quos quotque dari opo]rteat dato, iubetoque eum, sei ita pariat, condumnari popul[o], facitoque ioudicetur. sei condemnatus [erit, quanti condemnatus erit, praedes] ad q[uaestorem] urb[anum] det, aut bona eius poplice possideantur facito.

It is noticeable here that the proceedings are envisaged as *possibly* being completed through the mere *exigere* on the part of the prosecuting magistrate; but if the prosecutor demands it, the praetor (i.e. the principal magistrate) must appoint *recuperatores*; and the possibility of enforcement of the penalty by the public authority is envisaged only in a case where there has been a recuperatorial condemnation. Here a connection between *recuperatores* and official enforcement is quite evident; and, since the appointment of *recuperatores* is not indispensable, but depends on the special request of the prosecutor, one might conclude that *recuperatores* are thought of as appropriate only in cases where the prosecutor might apprehend resistance on the part of the defendant.

The second epigraphic source—the *lex agraria*[2] of 111 B.C.—also contains provisions about fines, and also speaks of the appointment of *iudices* or *recuperatores* by the magistrate. This

[1] 9 ff. [2] 30, 34, 35.

alternative appointment must have a concrete significance, and, although the passage is less informative than the *lex Latina tabulae Bantinae*, it is very easily accommodated in the hypothetical scheme which connects *recuperatores* with the public or official enforcement of fines. The same is true of the other two epigraphic sources, the *fragmentum Atestinum* of about 49 B.C. and the *lex Ursonensis* of 44 B.C. Those who are inclined to see in the recuperatorial procedure no more than the element of the 'public interest' being affected or involved in the issue under adjudication will of course rank these cases of fines exacted through *recuperatores* as a mere subordinate category of recuperatorial activity; but if one regards the element of official enforcement as central to the notion of *recuperatores*, then these cases about fines will present themselves as entirely typical: there is no advantage in prescribing a statutory penalty, if one has omitted to provide for its exaction.

If one continues to follow this conception of *recuperatores*, then their appearance in the administration of justice in the provinces—illustrated for us by the speeches of Cicero against Verres—is very easily explained. In order to evaluate their operation in this context, we must, however, keep in mind that Cicero represents Verres' administration of Sicily as corrupt and oppressive in the extreme; an administration under which there would never be any question of failure to enforce the government's wishes, against which the inhabitants of the province had absolutely no protection. In the second Verrine oration Cicero describes the taxation system which Verres set up in place of the ancient and traditional Hellenistic system, the *lex Hieronica*. According to Cicero, the tax-collectors were able to levy any amount they wished; they could exact the levy themselves, and if a Sicilian farmer had any complaints against the tax collection, he was obliged to appear in the role of plaintiff, rather than as defendant (which would have been the more natural position). Cicero speaks scornfully[1] of the clause in Verres' edict which promised the appointment of *recuperatores* in a case of dispute between tax-collector and farmer; according

[1] *Verr.* 2. 3. 35.

to him, the clause read: *si uter volet, recuperatores dabo*; but this, he says, concealed the true situation. Superficially, either party was free to demand the appointment of *recuperatores*, but of course the Sicilian farmer would never wish his case to be decided by Verres' appointees, whose judgment could be favourable only to the tax-collector.

This passage, up to now, has been interpreted in the sense that the farmer is unwilling to have such judges, because the bench of *recuperatores* would consist solely of the sycophantic favourites of the governor, before whom it would be a waste of time to raise objections to the tax; and as the justice over which Verres presided was extremely corrupt this explanation of the passage is entirely plausible. But on the other hand we ought to keep in mind that the whole episode is presented by Cicero as a monstrosity, and not merely because of the corruption of justice—no rarity in any case—but also because the usual relationship of plaintiff and defendant had been reversed. In the normal case—and here, I think, lies the key to understanding the role of *recuperatores* in fiscal litigation—the tax-collector would not simply seize the tithe himself by force, but would have to sue first in court for judgment for the amount.[1] In *this* case—i.e. the normal case—*recuperatores* would be the appropriate instance, as the official exaction of a settled sum due on a public liability (as in the fine cases) is already found associated with them. This is not in any way surprising, since the state must possess the means to recover revenue, or—where, as here, the tax-farming system prevails—must provide the tax-collectors with effective practical means of doing it. If this line of argument is correct, we see that it is not necessary to assume that all provincial justice normally operated with *recuperatores* irrespective of who was plaintiff and who defendant, because in the normal case the plaintiff was the tax-collector. It was merely to facilitate his exactions that *recuperatores* would have been necessary; and the contemptuous disregard for justice imputed by Cicero to

[1] Schmidlin, *Rekuperatorenverfahren* 62 ff.; D. 39. 4. 1. pr. (praetor's edict cited by Ulpian); Gaius, *Inst.* 4. 32.

Verres consisted precisely in the fact that the only recourse he offered the Sicilian farmers who had been actually plundered by the tax-gatherers was an action of the same nature—*recuperatorio iudicio*—against those who had robbed them.[1]

If we sum up what has now been said, the picture is as follows. We have observed that the special judicial category bearing the name *recuperatores* is most unlikely—to judge by the sources—to have arisen in the field of international disputes, and that it seems more likely that it originated within the domestic Roman judicial sphere. I advanced the hypothesis that the peculiarity of *recuperatores* is to be found in their appearance in public-law settings, in which one would, *a priori*, have admitted the likelihood of official enforcement of judgments; and it has been seen that this hypothesis is consistent, not only with those cases, but also with the passages in which disputes of a purely private-law nature are described. It remains to be seen whether the same is true of the other areas in which the operation of *recuperatores* is reported.

The first such area comprises what Schmidlin calls 'gemeingefährliche Delikte',[2] delicts involving danger to the public; these are the situations to which the following procedural remedies are attached: the *actio de hominibus armatis coactisve*, the *interdictum de vi armata*, the *actio vi bonorum raptorum*, and the *actiones de turba* and *de incendio ruina naufragio rate nave expugnata*; in addition, certain types of *iniuria*, particularly *iniuria* involving physical force; and, perhaps, certain situations arising from edictal provisions for reinforcing *in ius vocatio*. The general and probably correct opinion is that *recuperatores* appeared in all these different kinds of case. But why? What was the special feature of this judicial category, which made it appropriate for just these cases?

Again, the general view is that the special feature was the *speed* of recuperatorial procedure. Certainly, the procedure was a speedy one; *recuperatores* were not tied to the *rerum actus*, in other words they could sit on days when other court proceedings

[1] It was an action for the unheard-of *eightfold* value: as to this, see Kelly, *Roman Litigation* 171–2.

[2] Op. cit. 45.

were prohibited; moreover, they were regularly given a specific command by the praetor to pronounce judgment within a fixed time.[1] But is the rapidity of recuperatorial procedure really enough to explain the judicial category as such? Would it have really been impossible to appoint a *iudex unus* free from the *rerum actus* but told to reach an early verdict?[2] Were there not plenty of cases in purely private-law categories, perhaps above all in the field of commerce, in which a speedy judgment would have been of great importance to the plaintiff (or perhaps both parties)?

These questions throw strong doubt on the traditional explanation. The recuperatorial procedure may very well have been speedy, but wherever it appears in the area of 'gemeingefährliche' and similar delicts it is a much more natural assumption that, since in such cases—unlike the rest of private-law litigation—any plaintiff would by definition be dealing with a rough opponent, the *recuperatores* represent force rather than speed; that they reflect the willingness of the state to help him in the recovery and enforcement of judgment, since left to his own devices he might well be helpless. An indirect, but useful hint that this is the true reading of the recuperatorial role is the fact that we have unambiguous evidence that witnesses in recuperatorial cases were summoned officially.[3]

There remains the area of *causae liberales*, in which, at any rate in the Empire, *recuperatores* were used.[4] In the matter of *causae liberales* once more the weakness of the 'public interest originating in international relations' view of the *recuperatores* is seen. Schmidlin[5] sees the link between the archaic 'international' *recuperatores* and those operating later in the domestic

[1] Schmidlin, *Rekuperatorenverfahren* 130 ff.

[2] As to the *rerum actus*, see Behrends, *Geschworenenverfassung*, 158 ff.

[3] Below, pp. 58 ff.

[4] Juvenal 7. 115 ff. speaks of a hearing *dubia pro libertate* before a single judge. This text is I think the only one which suggests that a *liberalis causa* was so tried; but the *bubulcus iudex* mentioned by Juvenal might easily be a judge of the *cognitio*, as this satire belongs to the period of Trajan or even Hadrian, and is thus perhaps 70 or 80 years later than the edict of Claudius which evidently treats as general the jurisdiction of *recuperatores* in such cases.

[5] Op. cit. 83.

setting in the fact that an arbitral sorting-out of affairs after a war would involve freeing those reduced to slavery by capture, and re-enslaving those set at liberty; and he quotes the passage from the *lex Antonia de Termessibus*, cited above, in support: the *recuperatores* here were to ensure the recovery of whatever *leiberos servosve* the Termessians had lost. But *leiberos servosve* is only an exhaustive lawyer's way of saying 'people of whatever condition', and the text contains no suggestion that there is going to be an adjudication of the status of one category or the other; moreover, once the *causae liberales* arose in the purely domestic jurisdiction it would surely be extremely far-fetched to entrust their adjudication to a multiple court just because of one of the known functions of a court of this kind on the international plane. Why could a single judge not have done the job? And where is the 'public interest', supposed to lurk in all recuperatorial operations, in, say, a dispute as to whether a private citizen's will has or has not the effect of manumitting a particular slave?

If the matter is looked at, however, from the perspective now suggested—that *recuperatores* had coercive powers consequent upon their judicial powers—it will be seen that a well-marked problem in the general field of *causae liberales* is rationally and effectively met by the recuperatorial type of jurisdiction.

What, essentially, is a *liberalis causa*? Essentially, it is a contest in which one person stands to have his liberty declared—or denied—but, more interesting to the student of litigation, it is a contest in which the other party stands to gain or lose a most valuable form of property. Assuming, as seems fair, that the party asserting the *unfree* status of his opponent (or opponent's protégé) is typically in a stronger social and physical position[1] than the person whose status is in issue, the following alternative situations result: where the plaintiff is the party asserting the slave status of the other, no great problem will arise in carrying into effect a judgment favourable to himself; but where the roles are reversed, and the plaintiff is, or represents, the party seeking to have his own liberty declared as against another,

[1] Kelly, *Roman Litigation*, 61 ff.

we find a classical type of plaintiff-disadvantage[1] and one in which, if the public *favor libertatis*[2] is to be made effectual, a reinforced procedure is necessary.

Several passages from the Digest title on freedom conferred by *fideicommissum* illustrate a simple problem facing a slave whose owner wished him to be freed after his own death, namely the avoidance by the fideicommissary of his duty by lying low (*latitare*) and keeping out of the reach of legal action. I am not sure why this topic should be found concentrated in the title *De fideicommissariis libertatibus*, because presumably a similar problem must have existed where a slave was directly freed by will, thus imposing upon the heir or legatee the obligation of physically releasing him; no doubt it is an accident of compilation. At any rate, we are given in D. 40. 5. 26. 7 the actual words of the *senatusconsultum Rubrianum* (A.D. 103):

Si hi, a quibus libertatem praestari oportet, evocati a praetore adesse noluissent, si causa cognita praetor pronuntiasset libertatem his deberi, eodem iure statum servari, ac si directo manumissi essent.

(These words are introduced by Ulpian with the sentence *subventum libertatibus est senatus consulto . . . in haec verba.*) This text is taken[3] to mean that the *senatusconsultum* applied only to 'fideicommissary liberty overdue' (as Buckland put it), presumably because Ulpian says, further on,[4] *hoc senatusconsultum ad omnes pertinet latitantes, quos fideicommissam libertatem praestare oportet*; but it will be seen that the actual words of the *senatusconsultum* say nothing of such a limitation, and I can see no reason for not taking the *senatusconsultum* as applying to all cases, fideicommissary or otherwise, in which *libertas praestari oportet*. Ulpian must therefore be understood as meaning that the *senatusconsultum* applies to fideicommissary liberty *as well*,

[1] Kelly, *Roman Litigation*, 61 ff.

[2] Gaius, *Inst.* 4. 14; Kaser, *RZPrR* 61, 74; though Watson, *Persons*, 207, 217 is doubtful whether the doctrine of *favor libertatis* was well developed in the Republic.

[3] Buckland, *The Roman Law of Slavery*, 612.

[4] D. 40. 5. 26. 10.

of course, as to non-fideicommissary cases. The point about the *senatusconsultum*, then, is that direct summoning by the praetor (according to Kaser,[1] on the application of the slave himself without an *adsertor*, though this is not clear) is exceptionally used in this case—at a period when direct intervention by magistrates in instituting civil proceedings or in enforcing judgments had still not become general. This suggests to me that the question of freedom was always regarded as a special case requiring special remedies, and it is not surprising, then, if the peculiar character of *recuperatores* is taken to be the element of enforcement as well as adjudication, that *causae liberales* are found within the area of their jurisdiction.

To the whole theme of this treatment of the *recuperatores* the objection must naturally remain that no direct evidence seems to exist in the sources which would actually show us the *recuperatores* exercising a coercive as well as a purely judicial function; and that this objection is a powerful one cannot be denied. Nevertheless, there is at least one text in which the judicial operation of *recuperatores* and the actual carrying out of their judgment are in such close juxtaposition as to raise a fairly strong inference that the judicial and executive operations were in the hands, or under the control, of the same people. This is a passage from the speech in which Cicero claims the right to prosecute Verres;[2] the context is Cicero's account of the efforts of a Sicilian woman called Agonis, formerly a slave of Venus of Eryx, to regain property, taken from her by an officer of a Roman general, by claiming (as was there usual) that the property belonged to Venus.

Ubi hoc quaestori Caecilio, viro optimo et homini aequissimo [ironic], nuntiatum est, vocari ad se Agonidem iubet; iudicium dat statim 'si paret eam se et sua Veneris esse dixisse'. Iudicant recuperatores id quod necesse erat; neque enim erat cuiquam dubium quin illa dixisset. Iste in possessionem bonorum mulieris intrat; ipsam Veneri in servitutem adiudicat; deinde bona vendit, pecuniam redigit.

Now Caecilius is himself a magistrate, the magistrate who

[1] Op. cit. 379. [2] *Div. in Caecilium* 55 ff.

appoints the board of *recuperatores*. But note that, on foot of their judgment, no further formalities seem necessary for him; he enters[1] on the property of Agonis, and this is represented by Cicero as being a simple consequence of the judgment of the *recuperatores*. (The outrageousness of his behaviour lay, not here, but in forcing upon Agonis a formula which was unrealistic.) As for the physical problems of seizing property, these naturally would present no difficulty (especially against an impoverished female ex-slave) to a magistrate with a staff of constables; but, if it seems probable (as I suggest) that the recuperatorial judgment enabled immediate official enforcement to be carried out, as here, the constables would equally have been capable of acting, at the magistrate's order, in the interest of a private plaintiff. Relevant here—although not documented in the sources in an instance where they were actually used—must have been the powers of *vocatio* and *prensio* of which, Gellius tells us, Varro wrote an account.[2]

The mention of magistral *vocatio*, moreover, recalls one of several features of the recuperatorial jurisdiction, as it emerges from the sources, which strengthen rather than weaken the hypothesis which has been here put forward. The first and most telling of these is the well-documented association of *recuperatores* with the official summoning of witnesses, i.e. the attendance of witnesses actually compelled by the magistrate appointing the *recuperatores* rather than left to their own inclinations or the persuasions of the plaintiff. The second is the very curious listing of recuperatorial actions as *iudicia imperio continentia*.[3] The third is the relation between recuperatorial jurisdiction and *infamia*. Finally, there is an interesting argument, even though one *ex silentio*, in the Digest texts on execution of judgments.

[1] My interpretation of this passage is based on the reading *intrat*, found in some MSS., rather than *mittit*, which is found in others. The Oxford, Teubner, Budé, and Loeb editions prefer *intrat* (Orelli has *mittit*), and in fact *mittit* would seem extremely awkward, as there is no adjacent object.

[2] *N.A.* 13. 12. 6. He cites Varro: *In magistratu habent alii vocationem, alii prensionem, alii neutrum; vocationem, ut consules et ceteri qui habent imperium; prensionem, ut tribuni plebis et alii qui habent viatorem; neque vocationem neque prensionem, ut quaestores et ceteri qui neque lictorem habent neque viatorem.*

[3] Gaius, *Inst.* 4. 105.

The official summoning of witnesses in a recuperatorial proceeding is attested beyond all doubt by c. 95 of the *lex Ursonensis*, a sort of combination of town charter and by-laws for the *colonia genetiva Julia* in Spain (44 B.C.). This chapter expressly deals with *recuperatores*, though without specifying the kind of case on which they might sit; and while the general tenor of the *lex* is a public-law one, suggesting that the *recuperatores* adjudicated on liability to the fines which the *lex* prescribes for various infractions, it is clear from a clause within the chapter that the procedure might be set in motion by an individual (*si privatus petet*, etc.). With regard to witnesses, the chapter says:

Testibusque in eam rem publice dumtaxat hominibus XX, qui coloni incolaeve erunt, quibus is qui rem quaeret volet, denuntietur facito. Quibusque ita testimonium denuntiatum erit quique in testimonio dicendo nominati erunt, curato uti at it iudicium adsint.

Note that the magistrate, in a proceeding which an individual can initiate, is not only to have a summons delivered to the witnesses (*denuntietur facito*), but is to make sure that they actually attend (*curato uti adsint*). It is true that the *si privatus petet* clause follows these provisions, but the only apparent way in which this is material is that special provisions are made for the case in which the *privatus* himself fails to show up at the hearing. There is nothing to suggest that the preceding parts of the chapter, which contain the rules about enforcing witness-attendance, did not apply to a case instituted by a *privatus* as well as to one instituted by the magistrate.[1]

Kaser, while naturally agreeing that recuperatorial proceedings are found associated with the official summoning of witnesses, says[2] that this is not proved for civil cases (and I readily admit that the whole context of the *lex Ursonensis* is administrative, so to speak, rather than civil law). On the other

[1] The *lex Mamilia* (*lex Iulia agraria*) of (?) 109 B.C. also contains both public summoning of witnesses and the public exaction of fines in the case of removal of boundary marks. It speaks of the official called *curator* having in such cases the *iuris dictio reciperatorumque datio addictio*. See also Schmidlin, *Rekuperatorenverfahren* 126 ff.

[2] *RZPrR* 145 n. 73.

hand, it seems to me that a source which Kaser himself refers to without citing[1]—Probus, *De litteris singulis fragmentum* 5. 8—almost certainly proves that the official summoning of witnesses in recuperatorial cases was known in the civil law, or at any rate in a context so nearly 'civil' as to make it impossible to draw any line on the far side of which official summoning would seem unlikely. This text come from a section of Probus' work on abbreviations devoted to abbreviations found *in edictis perpetuis*, and the abbreviation in question reads: Q.E.R. E.T.P.I.R.D.T.Q.P.D.T.D.D.P.F. Probus says this expands to the following clause (which, in order to justify a conventional abbreviation, must have been reasonably common): *quanti ea res erit, tantae pecuniae iudicium recuperatorium dabo testibusque publice dumtaxat decem denuntiandi potestatem faciam.* Of the other abbreviations in this section, all could easily belong to pure civil-law settings, and some have an unmistakable civil-law ring: V.B.A. (*viri boni arbitratu*); I.C.E.V. (*iusta causa esse videbitur*); N.C.C. (*non calumniae causa*); F.C. (*fraudare creditores* or *fiduciae causa* or *fidei commissum*). The probability seems to me strong that the abbreviation we are interested in does, in fact, refer to *recuperatores* in the settings where they might expect to be found in the edict—some forms of *iniuria*, delicts of public violence, etc.[2]

Apart from what I call this strong probability, there is a small but attractive hint in Cicero's speech *pro Caecina* 28 that in that very case, which was tried by *recuperatores*, the edictal provision mentioned by Probus was operated. The foundation of the trial was that *P. Dolabella praetor interdixit, ut est consuetudo, de vi hominibus armatis*,[3] and Cicero goes over in his speech the evidence of the witnesses called for his opponent. He names them one after the other, with comments on what they have had to say. But after the first and second, he does not refer to their numerical sequence until he comes to the last of them. Then he calls him *decimo vero loco testis exspectatus et ad extremum reservatus*—'the witness we have been waiting for, called in tenth place and thus kept to the last'. It strikes me

[1] *RZPrR* 145 n. 73. [2] Schmidlin, *Rekuperatorenverfahren* 96. [3] *pro Caecina* 23.

that if the number ten had been without any special significance, it would scarcely have been mentioned, unless Cicero had been counting all the rest as well—third, fourth, fifth, etc.—which he did not do; and I think it is not far-fetched to bring this passage into juxtaposition with the praetorian promise, evidenced by Probus, to take on the job of getting up to ten witnesses into court for a recuperatorial trial. If I am right about this, the promise meant that each party would have ten witnesses summoned for him, as the ten mentioned by Cicero were all his opponent's. Whether the hypothetical total of twenty witnesses might then be related to the twenty witnesses in the administrative prosecutions of the *lex Ursonensis* (which belongs to much the same era as the *pro Caecina*) may remain an open question.

As to the purpose of official summoning of witnesses: it can only have had the object of making sure that reluctant witnesses actually attended and spoke up; even at the present day, persons not directly concerned with trouble are usually glad enough not to be brought into it. Note also that one of the witnesses who gave evidence on the side of Cicero's opponent in Caecina's case apparently did so little service to his side that Cicero went out of his way to thank him for his honesty.[1]

The bearing of all this on the theory that *recuperatores* not only pronounced judgment but also enforced it is evident. A departure from the ordinary notion (that a litigant brings his own witnesses), if established in cases which notoriously are ones involving the public interest, seems to me to give colour to the idea that in these same cases, and for the same reasons, the ordinary notion that a litigant must enforce his own judgment was departed from.

Some words must now be said on the subject of the *iudicia imperio continentia*, a category to which Gaius[2] assigns recuperatorial cases and which he contrasts with the category of *iudicia legitima*. The words of Gaius are as follows:

Imperio vero continentur recuperatoria, et quae sub uno iudice

[1] Ibid. 26. [2] *Inst.* 4. 105.

accipiuntur interveniente peregrini persona iudicis aut litigatoris. In eadem causa sunt quaecumque extra primum urbis Romae miliarium tam inter cives Romanos quam inter peregrinos accipiuntur. Ideo autem imperio contineri iudicia dicuntur, quia tamdiu valent quamdiu is qui ea praecepit imperium habebit.[1]

In spite of Gaius' explanation of why *iudicia quae imperio continentur* are so called, the classification of actions as between these and *iudicia legitima* has been something of a puzzle. On the one hand, it might seem evident that some material reason underlay the distinction. On the other hand, Bonifacio[2] denies any dogmatic basis for the distinction, says that *legitima* implies, not that an action is grounded on a statute, but that it has been regulated by a particular statute, to wit the *lex Julia iudiciorum privatorum*, and that the distinction, which is not mentioned anywhere before the *lex Julia*, reflects merely the reorganization by which *legis actiones* were practically abolished: henceforth the *iudicia* which used to carry the *legis actio* procedure are called *iudicia legitima* by reference to the *lex* which effected the reform. As to the time limits mentioned by Gaius for both types of *iudicium*,[3] he says that the *iudicia* not characterized as *legitima* are not limited in time *for the reason* that *imperio continentur*, but (a subtle distinction) they are 'said' to *imperio contineri*, because as a matter of fact they do not survive the magistrate's term of office.

The point that concerns us here is left untouched by Bonifacio, Kaser,[4] Behrends,[5] and all the others, namely: what is the reason for the disposition, whether resulting from the *lex Julia* or not, by which *iudicia recuperatoria* (and others)[6] are 'bounded' by the *imperium* of the magistrate authorizing them? Why are they thus 'bounded' in time (as Gaius tells us), and does this confinement reflect anything of a deeper material or functional containment? Even to pose this question, given the

[1] See also *Inst.* 4. 109.

[2] *Studi Arangio-Ruiz*, ii. 207 ff.

[3] See also Bonifacio, 142 *Archivio Giuridico* 34 ff.

[4] Op. cit. 116.

[5] Op. cit. 34–5.

[6] Gaius, *Inst.* 4. 105, includes also cases in which the action is tried outside Rome, or in which the judge or either of the parties is a foreigner.

scarcity of our sources, is as much as to promise that any answer will be speculative. But if the question is brought close to the theoretical structure I have been trying to build, an answer immediately appears: *iudicia recuperatoria* are contained within the *imperium* for the very simple reason that they are part of its exercise; their connection with the 'command' function of the magistrate is more intimate than is the case with *iudicia privata*, in which, after directing an *unus iudex* to try the issue, the magistrate steps out of the picture; here, as we have seen, he enforces the attendance of witnesses, and (as I believe) the ultimate judgment of the court; and here, in the typical case, an issue is raised of a kind which, even if no litigant ever appeared to complain of his injuries, the public interest might require the magistrate to investigate, applying his *imperium* to it if necessary.[1]

Another matter which is worth adverting to briefly is the peculiar disgracefulness, from the defendant's point of view, of recuperatorial proceedings, if we may judge from Cicero's words in his speech *pro Caecina* (when it was not his client, but his client's opponent, who complained about the procedure used against him). Except for the *actio iniuriarum* (which could in some circumstances be heard by an *unus iudex*)[2] and the *actio vi bonorum raptorum*, there is no direct evidence that any action commonly tried by *recuperatores* was an *actio famosa* in the strict sense.[3] Yet it clearly was felt as a procedure most wounding to the reputation, probably because the usual defendant was charged with behaviour which, if not criminal, verged upon the criminal, but probably also because—for that very reason—it was equipped with very direct modes of enforcement, most unbecoming to the dignity of the defendant, if he had any dignity. Here is what Cicero says, in answer to the defendant's

[1] This interpretation of *imperio contineri* would of course have the same implication for the kinds of case mentioned in the preceding footnote.

[2] *Rhet. ad Her.* 2. 13. 19: two actual cases of *iniuria* are mentioned as having been decided by a single judge.

[3] Gaius, *Inst.* 4. 182, mentions as actions carrying *ignominia* for the unsuccessful defendant those on *furtum*, *vi bona rapta*, *iniuria*, *pro socio*, *fiducia*, *tutela*, *mandatum*, and *depositum*. See also Cic. *pro Caecina* 7–8.

grievance about being subjected to the *interdictum de vi hominibus armatis*:

Verumtamen nimiae vestrae benignitati pareremus, si alia ratione ius nostrum recuperare possemus. Nunc vero quis est qui aut vim hominibus armatis factam relinqui putet oportere, aut eius rei leniorem actionem nobis aliquam demonstrare possit? Ex quo genere peccati, ut illi clamitant, vel iniuriarum vel capitis iudicia constituta sunt, in eo potestis atrocitatem nostram reprehendere, quum videatis nihil aliud actum nisi possessionem per interdictum esse repetitam?[1]

The defendant is saying 'It is too bad of you to use this very severe procedure, so damaging to my good name—a procedure appropriate to acts on which criminal prosecutions might be based (of which of course there is no question of my being guilty).' Cicero is replying: 'We say you *are* guilty of such acts, which are admittedly grave enough to warrant criminal proceedings; but as we choose to stick to civil proceedings, why should we be reprobated for bringing the only kind of proceedings which seem to us adequate to the case? Can you point out any milder mode by which we might have secured our rights, since we are, after all, dealing with a case of organized and armed violence?' The kernel of what is in issue here (disregarding the facts of the case) is the severity[2] of the proceeding, and I feel that in spite of the lack of any reference to the form of the judgment, if Cicero's client wins, or the mode of its enforcement, the severity must lie in the latter element: Dolabella the praetor will personally see to it that Caecina's rights are restored. The defendant is therefore faced right from the start with the prospect of the sheriff's men, so to speak, with no decorous interval in which (if it were a *iudicium privatum*) the *actio iudicati* or *missio in possessionem* might be activated as a last resort if he failed to conform to the judgment. No wonder, then, in a world where even an oblique imputation of insolvency could ground an *actio iniuriarum*,[3] Caecina's adversary com-

[1] Cic. *pro Caecina* 9.

[2] It was not a *lenior actio* in the sense of the passage just cited or the immediately preceding passage.

[3] D. 47. 10. 15. 32 (Servius cited by Ulpian); 47. 10. 19 (Gaius).

plained about being involved in a *iudicium* which would imperil his reputation.

It is perhaps worth adding that a rudimentary hint of the 'unrespectable' nature of recuperatorial jurisdiction (at any rate from the defendant's point of view) lies in the name *recuperatores* itself. Obviously if the *recuperatores* judicially absolve the defendant, there is nothing to *recuperare*. Consequently if the judges bear this title before they even begin the hearing, there is the implication (the proleptic *recuperatio*) that the defendant will be condemned. To be at the defendant's end of a recuperatorial proceeding may have been, right from the start, wounding to the *existimatio*.

A final consideration worth advancing is founded on the Digest texts on the execution of civil judgments. If I were quite wrong about the *recuperatores*, i.e. if their judgments left the plaintiff in exactly the same position as if he had succeeded in getting his adversary condemned in a *iudicium privatum*, namely under the obligation (unless the defendant paid up) of instituting an *actio iudicati* or seeking a *missio in possessionem*, then one would expect to find somewhere, among the texts on execution of civil judgments, some reference to the steps necessary for a plaintiff to recover on a recuperatorial judgment in *iniuria* or in the 'gemeingefährliche Delikte', as Schmidlin and Kaser compendiously describe them. But if we turn to the Digest title 42. 1 *de re iudicata et de effectu sententiarum et de interlocutionibus* we find all possible kinds of judgments discussed *except* judgments in matters within the recuperatorial competence. There are texts on judgments in debt,[1] noxal actions on slaves' delicts,[2] *fideicommissa*,[3] *stipulatio*,[4] *depositum* and *commodatum*,[5] *pignus*,[6] the *actio pro socio*,[7] dowry,[8] gift,[9] the *actio rerum amotarum*,[10] and the *actio negotiorum gestorum*;[11] but not a word about judgments in *iniuria* or *vi bona rapta* or *vi hominibus armatis* or *liberalis causa* or proceedings brought by *publicani*. Of course this may be accidental; but to me it is yet another slight hint that the

[1] D. 42. 1. 4. 3.
[2] D. 42. 1. 4. 8.
[3] D. 42. 1. 5. 1.
[4] D. 42. 1. 11.
[5] D. 42. 1. 12.
[6] D. 42. 1. 15. 2 ff.
[7] D. 42. 1. 16.
[8] D. 42. 1. 20.
[9] D. 42. 1. 30.
[10] D. 42. 1. 52.
[11] D. 42. 1. 64.

*iudicia recuperatoria*, straddling the middle ground between purely *privata iudicia* and criminal proceedings officially initiated, had a built-in enforcement mechanism emanating directly from the *imperium* of the magistrate.

It is of course quite true that a conception of *recuperatoria iudicia* such as I have been trying to construct implies something of a foreign body in civil procedure—where as a rule the successful paintiff must enforce his own judgment—as well, incidentally, as a serious qualification of views which I have previously expressed.[1] But there is no need to think of the anomaly as being, quantitatively, of much significance in the life of Roman litigation. In the next chapter, on the statistics of Roman litigation, I shall be showing what a very insignificant part the whole law of delict seems to have played in the actual work of the courts and of the jurists concerned with court practice; in particular, the *iniuria* complex, even if augmented by the 'violent' praetorian wrongs, seems barely to have existed in litigious practice, so that the kind of case seen in Cicero's *pro Caecina* was of the utmost rarity (and for this reason, no doubt like treason trials in the modern common-law world, guaranteed to be a *cause célèbre* by virtue of its being brought at all). *Liberales causae*, indeed, were common enough, but these were in some ways a special case.[2] By and large, the acceptance of the theory here advanced as to the basic functional characteristic of the *recuperatores* as distinct from the *unus iudex* does not involve more than a quantitatively very minor adjustment in our general picture of Roman litigious practice.

At this point a brief consideration of the *decemviri stlitibus iudicandis* should be inserted. This element of the judicial structure of the Republic is in some ways obscure—there is no unanimity, for instance, on the question whether these *decemviri* are identical with the early plebeian *iudices decemviri*,[3] though modern opinion[4] seems to favour identity—but there is no doubt that at the end of the Republic the *decemviri*

1 *Roman Litigation*, 12 ff., 29.

2 See above, pp. 55 ff.

3 Livy 3. 55. 7; see Kaser, *RZPrR* 40 and n. 40 with literature; Behrends, *Geschworenenverfassung* 110; Schmidlin, *Rekuperatorenverfahren* 83.

4 La Rosa, 4 *Labeo* (1958) 15; Franciosi, 9 *Labeo* (1963) 170 ff.

exercised a jurisdiction in *liberales causae*, and that later, through a reform of Augustus, they were changed into something like a panel of presidents for the centumviral court.

There is the vexing problem of why a body of judges whose only apparent function was the decision of *liberales causae* should have carried such a title as *Xviri stlitibus iudicandis* (if *stlis* = *lis* in the later general sense) implying a completely general jurisdiction. On this point, satisfactorily answered by nobody, only hypotheses are possible. It may be that by the time for which we have hard evidence about the functioning of the *Xviri*, they had been stripped of most of an originally wider competence (by the expansion of the field of operation of the *unus iudex*?), or it may be that in archaic times, to which the form *stlis* belongs, the word had a specialized sense, afterwards lost, of a *person* whose status was in dispute. (Something like this happened with the word *arbiter*.) This suggestion might make more sense of the curious phrase *praedes litis et vindiciarum.*[1]

Whatever the truth about this, the Augustan reform is clearly evidenced by Suetonius[2] and Dio Cassius;[3] they tell us respectively that [*Augustus*] *auctor*... *fuit*... *ut centumviralem hastam quam quaestura functi consuerant cogere Xviri cogerent*; and [the XXvirate which under Augustus succeeded the XXVIvirate contained] *καὶ οἱ δέκα οἱ ἐπὶ τῶν δικαστηρίων τῶν ἐς τοὺς ἑκατὸν ἄνδρας κληρουμένων ἀποδεικνύμενοι.*[4] That these *decemviri* heard *liberales causae* is clear from Cicero:

Cum Arretinae mulieris libertatem defenderem, et Cotta decemviris religionem iniecisset non posse nostrum sacramentum iustum iudicari, quod Arretinis adempta civitas esset, et ego vehementius contendissem civitatem adimi non posse, decemviri prima actione non iudicaverunt; postea, re quaesita et deliberata, sacramentum nostrum iustum iudicaverunt.[5]

[1] See Kaser, *RZPrR* 73 n. 46.

[2] *Divus Augustus* 36.

[3] 54. 26. 6.

[4] There is, however, a problem even here, because Pomponius, D. 1. 2. 2. 29, says *deinde cum esset necessarius magistratus qui hastae praeesset, Xviri in litibus iudicandis sunt constituti*; a report which appears to refer, as the context shows, to the middle Republic; but the testimony of Suetonius and Dio Cassius is generally preferred to the Pomponius text which is taken to be either corrupt or mistaken: see Schmidlin, *Rekuperatorenverfahren* 85, and the literature there mentioned at n. 5.

[5] *pro Caecina* 97.

Also: *Quin etiam si decemviri sacramentum in libertatem iniustum iudicassent* . . .[1] There is then at first sight the problem of jurisdiction in *causae liberales* being exercised by *decemviri* as well as by *recuperatores*. La Rosa believed[2] that there was no genuine concurrence; the *recuperatores*, she thought, operated originally in the provinces in such cases, the *Xviri* at Rome, until under Claudius[3] all jurisdiction in *causae liberales* was given to *recuperatores*; in the interval between the Augustan reform and that of Claudius, jurisdiction in such cases was exercised by ten *iudices selecti*. The weakest part of this hypothesis is that which reads into the *oratio Claudii* more than a regulation in regard to the age of *recuperatores* and makes the speech the source of the whole transfer of jurisdiction. Schmidlin[4] seems to me to be nearer the mark when he refers the general recuperatorial jurisdiction in *causae liberales* to the same Augustan reform which switched the *Xviri* to the presidency of the *centumviri*.

Whatever the exact chronology of the development of recuperatorial jurisdiction in *causae liberales*, the point I have been trying to make—namely the coercive nature of the recuperatorial jurisdiction as such—harmonizes extremely well with its functional association with the *Xviri*.

These *Xviri* were minor magistrates—part of the XXVIvirate, then of the XXvirate[5]—but minor though they were, they had the means of making themselves felt. (The *tresviri capitales*, after all, were also part of the XXVIvirate, and they are taken[6] to have exercised a short-shrift criminal jurisdiction over the lower strata of the population, being themselves able to execute capital sentences.[7]) There is clear epigraphic evidence that a *decemvir* was equipped with subordinates; three inscriptions[8] show that *decemviri* had messengers (*apparitores*, *viatores*); and

1 *De domo sua* 78.

2 Op. cit. 19 ff.

3 She uses BGU 611 (the *oratio Claudii*) to prove this.

4 Op. cit. 87.

5 Dio Cassius 54. 26. 6–7.

6 Kunkel, *Kriminalverfahren* 71 ff., in this respect not contradicted by Jones, *The Criminal Courts of the Roman Republic and Principate*.

7 Dio Cassius 54. 26. 6–7; D. 1. 2. 2. 30 (Pomponius).

8 *CIL* 10. 5917 = Dessau 1909; *CIL* 14. 3492 = Dessau 1938; Dessau 1911.

this instantly recalls the passage in Aulus Gellius[1] where magistrates with the power of arrest are defined as those who have a *viator*. Consequently, the *decemviri stlitibus iudicandis*, minor magistrates though they were, were essentially equipped with the means of physical coercion[2] which, as I have tried to argue above, is vital to an effective jurisdiction in matters involving free or unfree status; and if, as is the case, we find the *Xviri* being replaced in this area of jurisdiction by *recuperatores*, the conclusion that *recuperatores* were associated with the physical means of doing the same job seems a highly likely one.

Whether the recuperatorial coercion was exercised via the constables of the magistrate who appointed the court, or was enforced by the private servants or *familiae* of the *recuperatores* themselves, is impossible to say; but I am inclined to the former[3] idea. The evidence from the Republic about the actual enforcement of judgment by official means is extremely slight; but any evidence there is points to a magistrate's activity rather than to that of a purely judicial organ. Thus Cicero recounts in a letter[4] the exaction of a debt owed by a non-Roman community to a Roman as having been carried out *manu militari* in circumstances where only the governor of the province could have authorized such a measure; and in his prosecution of Verres[5] he describes a situation in which a plaintiff, creditor of

[1] *N.A.* 13. 12. 6; see above, p. 58 n. 2. See Kübler, *RE* 4. 2263; Mommsen, *Römisches Staatsrecht*³ i. 360.

[2] As well as sacrosanctity (Livy 3. 55. 7); this, as in the case of the tribunate, suggests personal intervention of a physical kind being perhaps resisted.

[3] Professor Kunkel has commented privately that the notion of a college of 'private' judges being able to use the magistrate's constables does not seem to fit into the basic principles of contemporary Roman public law; he thinks that, at most, the magistrate would himself have commanded enforcement on the strength of the recuperatorial judgment. The issue seems to me to boil down to the fairly marginal question, in practice, of whether the employment of constables was provisionally authorized at the outset of the proceedings, or required a further order in the event of condemnation. In either event I would not deny that this employment rests on the magistral *coercitio*, not on the *recuperatores* themselves. Professors Kaser and Kunkel also see *Div. in Caec.* 55 as evidence that the magistrate authorized enforcement after judgment, but this must rest on a textual reading which seems to me unlikely: see p. 58 n. 1 above. From *l. Lat. tab. Bant.* 11 I think one can scarcely say that enforcement was to be expressly ordered after judgment, rather than that it may have been provisionally authorized simultaneously with the appointment of *recuperatores*.

[4] *Ad Att.* 5. 21. 10.

[5] *Verr.* 2. 1. 73–4.

the town of Lampsacus, is put up to demand payment from the Lampsacenes. If this accuser, says Cicero, were to say all that Verres had told him to say, *per eiusdem istius lictores a populo pecuniam posset exigere*: the persons who would have physically executed the judgment would have been the lictors of Verres himself.[1]

[1] Professor Kaser is doubtful about any suggestion that the normal enforcement procedure of the formulary system—*actio iudicati, missio in bona*—whereby the successful plaintiff took the initiative, was excluded in favour of an enforcement by the *recuperatores* (or at any rate by the magistrate on foot of their judgment). The point seems to me to be that *recuperatores* are the typical weapon of the legal system for use against a defendant from whom the plaintiff himself, without the aid of public force, would have no hope of exacting the judgment. A 'concurrence' in enforcement between the plaintiff in person and the public force represented by the magistrate's constables therefore would scarcely arise in practice.

# III

# The Statistics of Roman Litigation

An inquiry into the structure of the civil judicature of the Roman Republic ought to include a consideration of a subject which has not yet been investigated: namely, the statistical picture of Roman litigation, the relative prominence or rarity, in a litigious setting, of the various departments of the civil law. If some conclusions can be reached here, they may be useful instruments in appraising the standing, in the Roman judicial complex, of one kind of court or another.

It is evident that the relative prominence of a legal institution in a textbook or a code—in Gaius or in the Digest, to take the most obvious Roman sources—will not necessarily be a reliable guide to its relative prominence in the context of litigation, because a variety of factors may easily depress or inflate the degree to which disputes in a particular field actually tend to be carried into court. What is meant by this can be seen if we look at a modern textbook against the background of the known facts of modern litigation. Two examples from *Salmond on Tort*[1] will do.

On the one hand, the law of defamation receives a very full treatment, occupying 54 pages, or nearly one-seventh of so much of the book as is devoted to individual torts as distinct from general principles. But this proportion would be a very misleading guide to a legal historian of the future trying to assess the relative commonness of actions for defamation in English (or in Irish) courts. If he used it to support the crude estimate that one tort action in every seven might have been for defamation, or that a judge trying tort cases might spend about one day in seven in hearing libel and slander actions, he would be wildly wrong. In fact, as we can observe easily,

[1] 16th edn. (1973), by R. F. V. Heuston.

defamation actions are quite rare; and a whole term might easily go by without a single such action being tried in the High Court or the Circuit Court at Dublin.

On the other hand, the law of negligence together with the (separately treated but materially related) law of dangerous premises, dangerous chattels, and the *Rylands* v. *Fletcher*[1] complex take up 157 pages in *Salmond*, i.e. about three-eighths of the 'special part'. This is of course a large proportion, and would lead the legal historian of the future to assign an important place in litigation to negligence and its offshoots. But if he assumed even a rough quantitative equality in proportion between academic treatment and litigious prominence, again he would go seriously wrong, this time in the opposite direction; because actions based on negligence are enormously more numerous than three in eight of all tort actions. In fact they much outnumber all other tort actions put together; and the Dublin Legal Diary showing causes listed for trial might easily disclose four or five judges of the High Court and Circuit Court doing nothing else for several consecutive days but hear actions grounded in some form of liability for negligence.

The interest of this lies in the fact that the academic treatment of a legal institution does not, and perhaps for its own purposes need not, point out the factors—economic, social, psychological—which affect it so as to depress or inflate its significance in litigation. These factors, in the case of the torts just mentioned, are obvious to our own contemporary eyes; but they might not be so easy for a legal historian of the future to identify, if his extra-legal materials for the present era were as scrappy as ours are for the era of the Roman Republic.

Negligence actions preponderate hugely today for three main reasons. The most obvious one is the progressive industrial revolution, filling up the inhabited world with machines and processes which expose persons and property to constant danger. A second reason, scarcely less obvious, is that recogni-

[1] The 'rule in *Rylands* v. *Fletcher*' imposes a strict liability (independent of negligence) on the occupier for the escape of any dangerous thing which he has brought on to his land.

tion of this danger has led to widespread insurance of potential tortfeasors; insurance partly voluntary and prudential, but partly also compulsory (as with our third-party motor insurance) in consequence of socially inspired legislation; this means that the real defendant, in a negligence situation, is usually an insurance company, which of course is a solid 'mark' for damages, but which—if the party covered is unsuccessfully sued by a poor plaintiff—may not trouble to attempt the recovery of costs, and this of course positively encourages litigation. Thirdly, a plaintiff in a negligence action has nothing much to fear from the course of the proceedings; even the most unfavourable evidence, even the most searching cross-examination is unlikely to reveal anything about his conduct more damaging than contributory negligence on his own part, which is not, in the general estimation of society, anything to be much ashamed of.

But if we turn to defamation, none of these factors appears; indeed, there are countervailing factors. A slander uttered, or a libel published by a poor man or a low-circulation pamphlet or bulletin, is not worth pursuing, because any substantial award of damages will probably not be recoverable in practice. People do not, as a rule, insure themselves against defamation judgments, so that insurance companies are not regularly in the picture.[1] Perhaps even more important, a man who feels injured by a defamatory statement may be reluctant to sue its author because he knows that, in the glare of publicity which defamation actions habitually attract, he may be made to appear in an unflattering or disgraceful light. The cross-examination to which he must submit may create the impression that what was said of him was deserved, or very nearly so. And similar considerations play a part in the relative rarity of actions for trespass to the person and seduction.

This excursus into modern legal conditions is intended merely to illustrate the proposition that relative prominence in

[1] When libel insurance is sought by an author, for instance, he is generally offered cover only up to a certain percentage of a possible claim, and is thus left personally at risk for a certain proportion—in order to make him extra careful not to provide material for a claim.

academic or even legislative exposition need not correspond to relative prominence in litigation, and that disproportions of prominence, as between these areas, may be accounted for by entirely or largely extra-legal factors—at any rate, factors extraneous to the particular legal institution involved. Applying this insight to Roman conditions, it is clear that it would be unsafe to measure probable shares of litigation, among various departments of law, by reference to the relative bulk of undifferentiated juristic material devoted e.g. in Gaius or the Digest to these departments; and that extraneous factors corresponding to (though of course not identical with) those noticed in a modern setting will have accounted for the relative frequency or rarity of litigation in one department or another. It now remains, firstly, to see whether there are any ways of measuring the litigious potential of the different parts of Roman private law, and secondly, to see whether such knowledge as we have of Roman society, in its bearing on litigation, would support such measurements as we might arrive at.

Given the sparseness and—for our purposes—the relative muteness of the material relating directly to the late Republic, there seems to be no alternative to using whatever Roman material of any era is available; and there is no incongruity in drawing on Justinian's Digest. Although the great bulk of it consists of excerpts from jurists who lived more or less three centuries later than our period, it seems legitimate to suppose that the broad social and economic settings of private life were much the same. Certainly, large-scale events like the gradual extension of Roman citizenship to virtually the whole population of the Empire, or the economic decline of the third century A.D. and the shift of the centre of political gravity away from Rome itself must have left traces, and significant ones, on private law and on private ligitation; but when all allowance has been made for these events, there still do not appear, in the first centuries of the Empire, any 'distorting' features (in the sense of new factors tending to depress or inflate the relative litigious prominence of a legal institution) at all comparable with the influence of the industrial revolution and the rise of insurance in modern times. Indeed, the clearest indication of the general stability of the broad social and economic background in the Roman world is the very fact that Justinian's compilers could still use, as the raw material for a code for their own day, legal writings between 300 and 600 years old.[1] The fact that they were authorized to adapt this material to suit their own times is a poor answer to this argument for the slow rate of broad-spectrum social and economic change in antiquity; we can conceive the despair of a modern codifying commission asked to compile a code of common law for modern use from material some of it going back to the reign of Edward III and none of it later than that of Charles II. Even the most explicit authority to 'adapt' this material would not make their task much less hopeless.

If, then, it is legitimate to use the Digest for our purposes, it offers three lines of approach: firstly, an analysis of the distribution of *responsa* between different legal fields; secondly, a similar analysis of the distribution of *rescripta*; and thirdly, an analysis of the (much smaller) body of cases, presented neither in the form of *responsa* nor in that of *rescripta*, in which circumstantial features (such as genuine proper names), or a reference to an imperial *decretum*, or the positive statement that the case really occurred (e.g. '*ex facto scio* . . .'), point to an actual dispute having taken place.

(1) *Responsa*. It is not easy to decide how this subject should be approached, because of the considerable disagreement between modern scholars as to the significance of the word *responsum* or the various parts of *respondere* where they are encountered in the Digest. Thus, while the traditional view is that

[1] Professor Kaser has privately suggested that, despite these broad considerations, there were elements in the world of Justinian's compilers which might have distorted the quantitative picture in their selection of classical texts: e.g. the existence of a Christian rather than the pagan law of marriage. Of course I agree that this is so. Equally I would not dispute another point he makes: that the gap between the Republic and the classical period, in terms of the social substratum of the law, is not at all as great as that between the classical period and Justinian. But how to find a formula for readjusting a statistical pattern in conformity with these observations? I think it is best simply to bear them in mind when any particular conclusion is being based on the results of a statistical survey.

these words are a signal that a problem arising in litigation (actual or prospective) is involved, in other words that a *responsum* corresponds with a modern barrister's 'opinion' given on a client's actual problem,[1] there is also the view, represented by Schulz,[2] that 'the problematic literature [in the Digest] undoubtedly does contain a large number of *responsa* in the strict technical sense, but they are distinguishable by no sure criterion. "*Respondere*" is not decisive, since the word might be used of a letter answering a theoretical question; indeed a jurist might use it of his answer to a question raised by himself.' Kunkel's view[3] is more modest: he believes *responsum*, *respondere*, etc. did not necessarily mean opinions given by a jurist with the formal *ius respondendi* (a view with which one would have no difficulty in agreeing), but he does not repeat Schulz's statement, for which Schulz himself produces no supporting evidence, that behind a view introduced by *respondere* we may have a purely speculative or academic question, not raised in connection with actual or prospective litigation (and therefore useless for a statistical survey of litigation).

In fact, there are one or two strong indications which tell against Schulz, and which make an investigation of the *respondere* passages likely to be useful. First there is the well-known passage from Pomponius[4] (the latter part of it controversial on account of the problems surrounding the *ius respondendi*). Part of it reads:

Et, ut obiter sciamus, ante tempora Augusti publice respondendi ius non a principibus dabatur, sed qui fiduciam studiorum suorum habebant, consulentibus respondebant: neque responsa utique signata dabant, sed plerumque iudicibus ipsi scribebant, aut testabantur qui illos consulebant.

From these and the surrounding words the use of *respondere* in a strict, technical sense is evident, and the connection with litigation emerges in *iudicibus*. Anyone sharing Schulz's point of view would have to explain how, at the outset of the Digest,

[1] Thus, e.g. Kaser, *RPR* 28.

[2] *Roman Legal Science*, 224–5.

[3] *Herkunft u. soziale Stellung der römischen Juristen*, 283 and n. 598.

[4] D. 1. 2. 2. 49.

and in a passage by common consent[1] heavily interpolated—one, in other words, to which the compilers had paid special attention—*respondere*, if it really included speculative and academic opinions, could have been used in a clearly practical setting without qualifying words showing that here, at any rate, only litigious opinions were in mind.

A further factor is this: of the many thousands of sentences in the Digest which have a hypothetical form ('Si . . . etc.') scarcely a single one[2] uses any part of *respondere* as a means of introducing the jurist's solution to the point proposed. There are a very few passages in which *respondere* is used in a mood or tense clearly provisional (e.g. *respondebitur*,[3] *respondebimus*,[4] or *respondendum est*, *erit*[5]); but in nearly all the *si* passages anything like *respondeo* or *responderem* or *respondendum censeo* is avoided. Moreover, a very large number of views in the Digest are introduced by neutral verbs of opinion or expression such as *existimo*, *puto*, *dixi*, *scripsit*, etc., and the whole style of such passages differs conspicuously from those in which *respondere* occurs. The latter usually begin with a statement not in the conditional but in the indicative mood, with a fairly terse answer appended; and this suggests a difference in kind—of which *respondere* is the signal—between the settings in which the legal questions were asked. And since *respondere*, even in Schulz's meaning, does at least include the specialized sense of giving an opinion on a legal problem actually arising in real life, it seems a fair working assumption that what we have in the *respondere* passages is basically a reflection of real or potential litigation. Even if there might not be agreement on every such passage—and even if, as is certain, much of the apparently speculative *si* material also grew out of real litigious problems—it could be well admitted that the *respondere* corpus within the Digest

[1] Daube, 67 *ZSS* (1950) 511; Honoré, *Gaius* 82.

[2] D. 9. 3. 5. 12, 15. 1. 38. 1, and 40. 4. 48 are I think the only cases of *si* used to introduce the problem with the commonest form (*respondit*) used to answer it. In D. 23. 3. 71 and 28. 2. 2 *si* is used with the rather unspecific and rare answer *respondetur*.

[3] As in D. 2. 11. 4 pr.

[4] As in D. 35. 2. 87. 3.

[5] As in D. 5. 4. 10, 28. 6. 25. Other provisional forms: *respondere melius est* (D. 50. 17. 85. pr.); *quod vere responderetur* (D. 20. 5. 12. 1).

represents, by and large, and certainly in a bulk adequate for statistical use, reality rather than speculation.

In what follows, no use has been made of passages merely because the origin ascribed to them is a work of *responsa*; it is quite possible that, in order to clear up ancillary points of doubt which had occurred to him after dealing with a real problem, and to fill out unexplored corners, a jurist whose book consisted, in the main, of *responsa* in the technical sense and was therefore so entitled, might sometimes interlard the actual *responsa* with statements resulting from his own reflection and application of principle in the abstract. Accordingly, for present purposes only those passages are used in which some part of the verb *respondere* appears.

The main problem in presenting a statistical survey of *responsa* is how to group the various branches of private law, and clearly there is a danger here of preconceived notions dictating the scheme of grouping. But leaving this danger aside for the moment, it is permissible to begin by *excluding* certain classes of *responsa* from consideration.

The first and most obvious class to be excluded is that of *responsa* whose relevance is to criminal law only. Of this category, the Digest contains, on my count, 35 instances.[1] The possibility must not be overlooked that *responsa* found in 'private-law' parts of the Digest may have been given in connection with a case which arose via a criminal prosecution; but such cases are probably a small minority, and here, as elsewhere, it is permissible to stick to the overt circumstances of the *responsum* for statistical purposes, taking it as a fair assumption that false attributions of *responsa*, of the kind just envisaged, will probably cancel each other out as between the various parts of the Digest.

A second class obviously due for exclusion is that which can be broadly labelled 'public law'; legitimate subdivisions of this would be fiscal law, military law, and 'local government' or

[1] D. *48*. 1. 14; 2. 18; 5. 12 (11). 3, 5, 7, 9, 10, 12, 13; 5. 40 (39). pr., 4, 6, 8; 5. 41 (40). pr., 1; 5. 44 (43); 10. 14. pr.; 10. 16. pr., 1; 10. 24; 15. 5; 16. 1. 4, 10, 13; 16. 5; 16. 17; 18. 4; 18. 17. 3; 19. 34. pr., 1; 19. 43. 1; *49*. 1. 18; 1. 23. 2; 1. 24. pr. 1.

'police' law. The exclusion of such *responsa* will, on my count, take away a further 37 from the total.[1]

Thirdly, *responsa* dealing with procedure and with status in litigation can be excluded, not because they do not arise in connection with private-law disputes, but because, in most cases, it is impossible to make out the part of the territory of private law in which the procedural point arose. These cases can be classified as neutral and left out of the reckoning; they are not, in any case, very numerous (on my count, there are 36 of them).[2] In some few procedural cases the original area of substantive law is, in fact, visible; and these are retained in the count.

Having made these exclusions, we are left, on my count, with a total of 1,306 *responsa*, on topics ranging from *furtum* to *fideicommissa*, from the *lex Aquilia* to the *SC Velleianum*. It would be pointless and misleading just to indicate, for instance, the number of *responsa* per subject—taking 'subject' as equivalent to Digest title—because in some parts of the Digest a succession of titles is much more closely linked together materially than in others. It seems better, even at the risk (already adverted to) of the arrangement being influenced by preconceived ideas, to group the *responsa*, not under individual titles, but in larger masses corresponding to the broad areas of life in which the litigation, actual or potential, represented by the *responsa* is located.

For the ultimate purpose of this chapter—an attempted assessment of the relative prominence of *centumviri*, *recuperatores*, and *unus iudex* in litigious life—it might be thought at first sight better to arrange the *responsa* according to the known fields of competence of these jurisdictions; but a moment's reflection will show that such a method is hopeless, as there is no way in

[1] D. *1*. 8. 8. 2; *2*. 14. 42; *4*. 6. 35. 9; *11*. 7. 6. pr.; *22*. 1. 43; *39*. 4. 15; *49*. 14. 28; 14. 38. pr., 1; 14. 39; 14. 50; 15. 5. 3; *50*. 1. 21. pr., 1, 2, 3, 4, 5, 7; 1. 36. pr., 1; 2. 2. 2; 2. 3. 2; 2. 10; 5. 5; 5. 9. 1; 7. 9 (8). pr., 2; 7. 10 (9); 7. 13 (12); 7. 18 (17) [two]; 9. 6; 12. 5; 12. 10; 16. 203; 17. 191.

[2] D. *2*. 4. 15; 4. 16; 8. 14; *3*. 2. 2. 5; 2. 4. pr.; 2. 13. 7; 2. 21; 3. 64; 3. 76; *5*. 1. 24. 2; 1. 49. 1; 1. 76; 1. 80; *11*. 1. 20. 1; 12. 2. 41; *42*. 1. 27; 1. 28; 1. 41. pr.; 1. 42; 1. 43; 1. 44; 1. 60; 1. 62; 1. 64; 4. 7. 13, 17; *44*. 1. 10; 1. 11; 2. 3; 2. 31; 7. 29; *49*. 1. 10. 3; 8. 2. pr., 1; 8. 3. pr., 1.

most cases of being certain that the concrete litigation, actual or prospective, which evoked the individual *responsum* really would have come before one of these jurisdictions rather than another. If, however, the *responsa* are grouped in large masses corresponding to broad areas of life, it will be possible to draw some conclusions, based on probability, as to the relatively greater degree of involvement of the respective jurisdictions in one such area or another.

A final preliminary point before presenting the figures: many *responsa*, perhaps about a sixth or a seventh of the total, deal with problems in which two areas 'overlap'. For example, D. 3. 5. 25 (26) contains a *responsum* on a problem about an action by an heir against one who *negotia gessit* for the deceased. The immediate problem occasioning the *responsum* concerned the extent of compensation recoverable in the *actio negotiorum gestorum* (triable by an *unus iudex*); but the plaintiff was a *heres legitimus* who had been so declared only as a consequence of the deceased's will having been found void in a judicial proceeding, which, in the Republic and early Empire, would very likely have been centumviral. Should the case be listed in such a way as to enlarge the contract/quasi-contract mass (where the *unus iudex* was predominantly, if not exclusively, active) or the succession mass (where, on the other hand, the *centumviri* were prominent)? In this particular case, where it is clear that two separate litigious operations are respectively reported and envisaged, I ought in theory to rank the *responsum* as of double value, so to speak, and award a point to each mass; but unfortunately the great bulk of the 'overlap' cases are much less explicit and do not permit even a guess as to whether one field or the other was the focus of the actual litigation. There is no alternative, therefore, in my particular exercise, to adopting a crude rule of thumb, whatever violence it may produce in particular instances; and, as the majority of 'overlap' cases are ones in which the area of succession is linked with some other area, I have simply added all such cases to the succession total, thus admittedly inflating it slightly by comparison with the others, so that the example just given is ranked (very perversely, I admit, in its own special circumstances) as evidence of litigation about inheritance rather than about quasi-contract. But with the exception of three cases[1] where there is a contract/delict overlap, all the other overlaps occur *within* a particular broad field (e.g. D. 17. 1. 59. 4: both *mandatum* and *pignus* are involved, but both are within the 'contract/quasi-contract' group, so no problem arises).

On my count, the numbers of *responsa* in the principal areas of life and law are, in descending order of frequency, as follows:

Succession (including questions on wills, *fideicommissa*, legacies, manumission on succession, *donatio mortis causa*, etc.) 761[2]

[1] D. *13*. 6. 21. pr.; *19*. 2. 30. 2; *44*. 7. 34. 2.

[2] D. *2*. 14. 35; 14. 44; 15. 3. 1; 15. 14; *3*. 3. 70; 5. 25 (26); 5. 33 (34); *4*. 3. 32; 4. 7. 9; 4. 31; 4. 33; *5*. 1. 74. 2; 2. 6. 2; 2. 8. 5; 2. 8. 8; 2. 11; 2. 13; 2. 19; 2. 21. 1, 2; 3. 36. pr.; 3. 47; 3. 58; 4. 9; *7*. 1. 33. pr.; 1. 35 1; 1. 36. 1; 1. 54; 1. 58. pr., 1, 2; *8*. 1. 18; 2. 10; 2. 41. pr.; 3. 37; 5. 20. pr.; *10*. 2. 20. 7; 2. 30; 2. 35; 2. 36; 2. 38; 2. 39. pr., 1, 2, 4, 5; 2. 41; *11*. 1. 18; *12*. 6. 38 pr.; 6. 53; 6. 67. 4; *13*. 5. 31; 7. 39; *14*. 5. 7; *15*. 1. 54/58; *16*. 1. 19. 1; 1. 28. pr.; 1. 29. pr.; *17*. 1. 58. 1; 1. 59. 1; 1. 60. 1; 1. 62. pr.; 2. 71. 1; 2. 73; *18*. 4. 22; 5. 8; 5. 10. pr.; *19*. 1. 47; *20*. 5. 11/14; 6. 11; *21*. 2. 11. pr.; 2. 12; 2. 73; *22*. 1. 14. pr., 1; 1. 42; 1. 48; 3. 15; 3. 27; 3. 29. 1; *23*. 4. 29. 1, 2; *24*. 3. 44. pr., 1; 3. 46; *25*. 4. 4; *26*. 2. 27. 1; 2. 32. pr.; 2. 32. 2; 2. 34; 3. 11. pr./1; *27*. 4. 5; *28*. 1. 25; 2. 19; 2. 25. pr., 1; 3. 15; 3. 20; 5. 8. pr.; 5. 11; 5. 35. 3; 5. 45 (44); 5. 46 (45); 5. 47 (46); 5. 48 (47). pr., 1, 2; 5. 54 (53); 5. 62 (61); 5. 73 (72); 5. 79 (78). 1; 5. 86 (85); 6. 30; 6. 32; 6. 33. 1; 6. 34. pr.; 6. 39. 2; 6. 43. pr., 1, 2, 3; 6. 45. pr., 1; 6. 46; 6. 47; 6. 48. 1; 7. 27. pr., 1; 7. 28; *29*. 1. 17. 1; 1. 25; 1. 40. pr., 1, 2 [two]; 2. 45. 4; 2. 75; 2. 76. pr., 1; 2. 78; 2. 90. pr., 1; 2. 91; 2. 92; 2. 98; 5. 4; 5. 18; 5. 22; 5. 26; 6. 3; 7. 14. pr.; *30*. 5. 1; 11; 13; 30. 7; 34. 5; 58; 75. 1; 81. 2; 84. 10; 91. pr.; 96. pr.; 104. pr., 1; 104. 7; 108. 2; 123. pr., 1; *31*. 30; 33. pr., 1; 34. pr., 1, 2, 3, 5, 6, 7; 35; 41. 1; 45. pr.; 47; 68; 70. 2; 76. 2; 77. pr., 15, 17, 23, 26, 29, 31, 32; 78. 1; 82. pr.; 83; 84; 86. pr., 1; 87. pr., 1, 2, 4; 88. pr., 1, 2, 3, 4, 5, 6, 7, 8, 9, 10, 11, 12, 13, 14, 15, 16, 17; 89. pr., 1, 2, 3, 4, 5, 6, 7; *32*. 6. pr.; 30. pr., 1, 2; 32; 33. pr., 1, 2; 34. pr. [two], 1, 2, 3; 35. pr., 1, 2, 3; 37. pr., 1, 2, 3, 4, 5, 6, 7; 38. pr., 1, 2, 3, 4, 5, 6, 7, 8; 39. pr., 1, 2; 40. pr., 1; 41. pr., 1, 2, 3, 4, 5, 6, 7, 8, 9, 10, 11, 12, 13, 14; 42; 57; 60. 1, 2; 61; 62; 63; 68. pr.; 69. 1; 78. pr., 1, 2, 3; 81. 1; 83. 1; 85; 91. 3; 92. pr.; 93. pr., 1, 2, 3, 4, 5; 97; 100. 3, 4; 101. pr., 1; 102. pr. [two], 1, 2, 3; *33*. 1. 5; 1. 6; 1. 12; 1. 13. pr., 1; 1. 15; 1. 18. pr., 1; 1. 19. pr., 1, 2; 1. 20. pr., 1 [two]; 1. 21. pr., 1, 2, 3, 4, 5; 1. 22; 2. 15. 1; 2. 16; 2. 17; 2. 18; 2. 22; 2. 26. pr.; 2. 27; 2. 28; 2. 31; 2. 32. pr., 1, 2, 3, 4, 5, 6, 7, 8, 9; 2. 33. pr., 1, 2; 2. 34. pr., 1; 2. 35; 2. 36. pr./1; 2. 37; 2. 38; 2. 39; 3. 1; 3. 3; 4. 6. pr.; 4. 7. 3; 4. 9; 4. 11; 4. 12; 4. 14; 4. 16; 4. 17. pr., 1; 5. 15; 5. 21 [two]; 5. 22; 6. 16. pr.; 7. 6; 7. 7; 7. 12. pr., 6, 35, 38, 39, 40, 41, 42, 43, 45, 46, 47; 7. 13. 1; 7. 15. pr., 1; 7. 16. 1, 2; 7. 18. 4, 5, 6, 7, 9, 11, 13, 14; 7. 19. pr., 1; 7. 20. pr., 1, 2, 3, 4, 5, 6, 7, 8, 9; 7. 27. pr., 1, 2, 3, 4, 5; 7. 28; 8. 8. pr.; 8. 14; 8. 15; 8. 16. pr.; 8. 22. pr., 1; 8. 23. pr., 1, 2, 3; 8. 26; 9. 7; 10. 8; 10. 13; *34*. 1. 4. pr., 1; 1. 5; 1. 9. pr.; 1. 10. 2; 1. 11; 1. 12; 1. 13. pr., 1, 2; 1. 15. pr., 1, 2; 1. 16. pr., 1, 2, 3; 1. 17; 1. 18. pr., 1, 2, 3,

Contract (including quasi-contract, *donatio*, *operae libertorum*, *lex Rhodia de iactu*, etc.) 288[1]

4, 5; 1. 19; 1. 20. pr., 1, 2, 3; 2. 4; 2. 6. pr., 1, 2; 2. 13; 2. 15; 2. 16; 2. 18. pr., 1, 2; 2. 21. 2; 2. 31; 2. 32. 3, 4, 5, 7, 8, 9; 2. 35. pr., 1; 2. 36; 2. 37; 2. 38. pr., 1, 2; 2. 39. pr., 1, 2; 2. 40. pr., 1, 2; 3. 11; 3. 12; 3. 20. pr., 1; 3. 22; 3. 25; 3. 26; 3. 28. pr., 1, 2, 3, 4, 5, 6, 7, 8, 9, 10, 11, 12, 13, 14; 3. 31. pr., 1, 2, 3, 4, 5; 4. 19; 4. 25; 4. 30. pr., 1, 2, 3, 4; 4. 31. pr., 1, 2, 3; 5. 1; 5. 4 (5); 5. 5 (6). pr.; 5. 29 (30); 6. 1; 8. 1; 9. 13; 9. 14; 9. 16. pr.; 9. 18. pr., 2; 9. 19; *35.* 1. 6. 1 [two]; 1. 27; 1 28. pr., 1; 1. 31; 1. 36. pr., 1; 1. 40. 2 [two], 3, 4, 5; 1. 62. 2; 1. 66; 1. 67; 1. 72. 8; 1. 83; 1. 84; 1. 85; 1. 101. pr., 3; 1. 102; 1. 108; 1. 109; 1. 112. 3; 2. 1. 19; 2. 11. 4; 2. 14. pr., 1; 2. 15. 3; 2. 22. pr.; 2. 24. 1, 2; 2. 25. pr., 1; 2. 26. pr., 1; 2. 27; 2. 61; 2. 86; 2. 94; 2. 95. pr., 1, 2; *36.* 1. 3. 2; 1. 17 (16). 6; 1. 26 (25). pr.; 1. 28 (27). 14, 16; 1. 33 (32); 1. 46 (44). pr., 1; 1. 48 (46); 1. 50 (48); 1. 59 (57). 1, 2; 1. 61 (59). pr.; 1. 63 (61); 1. 64 (62). pr., 1; 1. 77 (75). pr., 1; 1. 79 (77). pr., 1; 1. 80 (78). pr., 1, 2, 3, 4, 5, 6, 7, 8, 9, 10, 11, 12, 13, 14, 15, 16; 1. 82 (80); 2. 6. 1; 2. 26. pr., 1; 2. 27. pr., 1; 2. 28; 2. 31; 3. 18. pr., 1, 2; *37.* 1. 15; 4. 13. 1; 4. 14. pr., 1; 4. 20. pr.; 5. 6; 5. 18; 6. 3. 6; 7. 6; 8. 3; 10. 6. 1, 6; 10. 7. 8; 10. 8. pr.; 10. 13; 10. 14; 11. 8. 4; 11. 11. pr.; 14. 12; 14. 18; 15. 3; *38.* 2. 20. 4; 2. 26; 2. 35; 2. 36; 2. 46; 2. 47. pr., 1, 2, 3, 4; 2. 48; 3. 1. 2; 4. 11; 5. 3. pr.; 8. 8; 8. 10; 13. 1; 16. 6; *39.* 6. 18. 2; 6. 21; 6. 23; 6. 28; 6. 42. 1; *40.* 1. 6; 1. 7; 4. 15; 4. 17. 1; 4. 18. pr.; 4. 21; 4. 22 [two]; 4. 29; 4. 44; 4. 48; 4. 51. pr.; 4. 53; 4. 54. pr., 1; 4. 59. pr., 1, 2; 4. 60; 5. 14 [two]; 5. 18; 5. 19. pr., 1; 5. 23. 2; 5. 39. pr., 1; 5. 40. pr., 1; 5. 41. pr., 1, 2, 3, 4, 5, 6, 7, 8, 9, 10, 11, 12, 13, 14, 15, 16, 17; 5. 47. 4; 5. 49; 5. 56; 9. 26; *42.* 2. 7; 5. 28; 6. 6. 1; 8. 23; *44.* 2. 30. 1; 4. 17. 1, 2, 3; *46.* 1. 24; 3. 101. pr.; *47.* 6. 6. 1; *48.* 10. 14. 2; *49.* 14. 3. pr.; 14. 9; 17. 16. pr.; *50.* 16. 105; 16. 116; 16. 146; 16. 171.

[1] D. *2.* 13. 4. 2; 14. 7. 2, 5; 14. 47. pr., 1; 15. 3. 2; *3.* 5. 20 (21). pr.; 5. 26 (27). pr., 1; 5. 29 (30); 5. 41 (42); *4.* 4. 16. 1; 4. 29. 1, 2; 4. 32; 4. 39. 1; 4. 47. pr., 1; 4. 50; 7. 11; 8. 21. 1; 8. 43; 8. 44; 8. 50; *5.* 1. 36. 1; 1. 49. pr.; *10.* 4. 19; *11.* 1. 22; *12.* 1. 17; 1. 22; 1. 36; 5. 4. pr.; 5. 5; 6. 36; 6. 38. 1; 6. 61; 6. 67. 1, 2, 3; *13.* 1. 19; 5. 24; 5. 26; 6. 5. 9; 7. 30; 7. 34; 7. 43. pr., 1; *14.* 1. 1. 5; 1. 7. pr.; 2. 2. pr.; 2. 4. 1, 2; 2. 6; 2. 7; 3. 20; 4. 12; *15.* 3. 16; 3. 20. pr., 1; 3. 21; *16.* 1. 16. 1; 1. 17. pr.; 1. 19. 5; 1. 28. 1; 1. 29. 1; 3. 24; 3. 26. pr., 1, 2; 3. 27; 3. 28; *17.* 1. 16; 1. 22. 10; 1. 33; 1. 34. pr.; 1. 38. pr.; 1. 59. 2, 3, 4, 5, 6; 1. 60. pr., 2, 4; 1. 62. 1; 2. 29. 2; 2. 52. 7, 9, 10, 16, 18 [two]; 2. 63. 9; 2. 71. pr.; 2. 73 [two]; *18.* 1. 20; 1. 39. 1; 1. 40. pr., 1, 2, 3, 4, 5; 1. 41. pr.; 1. 60; 1. 64; 1. 65; 1. 69; 1. 77; 1. 78. pr.; 1. 80. 2; 1. 81. pr., 1; 3. 6. pr., 1, 2; 3. 8; 5. 9; 5. 10. 1; 6. 9; 6. 12 (11); 6. 15 (14). 1; 7. 1; 7. 9; 7. 10; *19.* 1. 6. 4; 1. 13. 26; 1. 39 [two]; 1. 43 [two]; 1. 48; 1. 52. pr., 1, 2, 3; 2. 15. 4, 8; 2. 21; 2. 27. 1; 2. 29; 2. 30. pr., 1, 2, 3, 4; 2. 31; 2. 51. pr., 1; 2. 54. pr., 1, 2; 2. 60. 3; 2. 61. pr., 1; 4. 1. 1; 5. 23; 5. 24; *20.* 1. 26. pr., 1, 2; 1. 29. pr., 2; 1. 31. pr., 1; 1. 32; 1. 34. pr., 1, 2; 2. 10; 3. 4; 4. 9 pr.; 4. 12. 5; 4. 18; 4. 19; 4. 21. pr., 1; 6. 9. pr., 1; 6. 11; 6. 12. pr.; 6. 15; *21.* 1. 56; 1. 58. pr., 1, 2; 2. 29. pr.; 2. 39. pr., 3; 2. 44; 2. 46. 2; 2. 63. pr., 1, 2; *22.* 1. 11. pr.; 1. 12; 1. 13. pr., 1; 1. 15; 1. 25. 1, 2; 1. 41. 1, 2; 1. 47; 2. 6; 3. 4; 4. 3; *37.* 6. 11; *38.* 1. 26. pr., 1; 1. 45; 5. 12; *39.* 5. 2. 7; 5. 23. pr., 1; 5. 29. 1, 2; *42.* 8. 22; *44.* 3. 6. 1; 3. 12; 7. 23; 7. 61. pr., 1; *45.* 1. 64; 1. 102; 1. 105; 1. 107; 1. 108. pr.; 1. 113. pr., 1; 1. 115. 2; 1. 121. 1; 1. 122. pr., 1, 2, 3, 4, 5, 6; 1. 126. 2; 1. 132. pr.; 1. 134. pr., 1, 2, 3; 1. 135. pr., 1, 2, 3, 4; 3. 28. 4; *46.* 1. 19; 1. 21. 4, 5; 1. 38. 1; 1. 41. pr., 1; 1. 44; 1. 45; 1. 59; 1. 60; 1. 62; 1. 63; 2. 30; 3. 34. 5; 3. 38. 2; 3. 45. pr.; 3. 67; 3. 72. 3; 3. 76; 3. 84; 3. 88; 3. 89. pr., 1, 2; 3. 90; 3. 94. 3; 3. 98. 8; 3. 99; 3. 100; 3. 101. 1; 3. 102. pr., 1, 2, 3; 5. 10; 7. 7; 7. 20; 8. 5; 8. 23.

| | |
|---|---|
| Family law (including family status, marriage, divorce, *dos*, *tutela*, *cura*, gifts between husband and wife, *alimenta*, etc.) | 114[1] |
| Property (including possession, servitudes, law of neighbours and boundaries, usufruct, etc.) | 85[2] |
| Free/unfree status (including *liberalis causa*, *statuliberi*, manumission otherwise than on succession) | 33[3] |
| Delict and quasi-delict | 22[4] |

There are several conspicuous features of this table. Firstly, even allowing for the fact that—as explained above—a few dozen 'overlap' cases involving succession have been arbitrarily included with the pure succession figures, the preponderance of this category is extremely marked, even surprising. It accounts for over 58 per cent, or very nearly three-fifths, of the total body of all private-law *responsa* and therefore, if my premisses are correct, it could be concluded that well over half of all Roman litigation arose via problems connected with succession on death. Probably no greater contrast could be found between the litigation patterns of the ancient and of the modern world,

[1] *1*. 5. 11; 5. 22; *4*. 4. 39. pr.; *5*. 1. 42; *12*. 3. 8; 4. 7. pr.; *15*. 1. 38. 1; *22*. 1. 41. pr.; *23*. 2. 6; 2 26; 2. 40; 2. 65. 1; 3. 48. pr., 1; 3. 49; 3. 60; 3. 62; 3. 71; 3. 72. pr., 1, 2; 3. 79. 1; 3. 85; 4. 2; 4. 17; 4. 23; 4. 29. pr.; 4. 32. pr.; 5. 8; *24*. 1. 38. pr.; 1. 39; 1. 49; 1. 55; 1. 57; 1. 58. pr., 1, 2; 1. 64; 1. 66. pr., 1; 3. 22. 12; 3. 34; 3. 38; 3. 45; 3. 49. pr., 1; 3. 50; *25*. 3. 3. 4; 3. 7; *26*. 1. 12; 2. 29; 2. 30; 2. 32. 1; 5. 25; 5. 26; 6. 2. 5; 6. 3; 7. 21; 7. 32. pr., 1, 2, 3, 4/5, 6, 7; 7. 34; 7. 43. 1; 7. 46. pr., 1, 3, 4, 5, 6; 7. 47. pr., 1, 2, 3, 4, 5, 6, 7; 7. 56; 7. 57. pr., 1; 7. 58. pr., 1, 2, 3, 4; 7. 59; 8. 20; 8. 21; 9. 8; *27*. 1. 16; 1. 23. pr., 1; 1. 32; 1. 36. 1; 1. 37. pr., 1; 2. 4; 5. 3; 6. 6; 7. 8. 1; 8. 5; 8. 7; 8. 8; 9. 14; 10. 7. 3; *44*. 4. 17. pr.; *46*. 3. 45. 1; 3. 48; *49*. 1. 28. 2; *50*. 16. 221.

[2] D. *6*. 1. 57; 1. 58; 1. 59; 1. 61; 1. 67; *7*. 1. 12. 2; 1. 13. 2; 1. 23. 1; 1. 37; 1. 50; *8*. 1. 4. pr.; *8*. 2. 13. pr.; 2. 40; 2. 41. 1; 3. 29; 3. 30; 4. 5; 5. 8. 5; 5. 16; 5. 17. 2; 5. 18; 5. 20. 1 [two]; 6. 6. 1; *9*. 1. 5; *10*. 3. 5; 3. 6. 4; 3. 26; *12*. 2. 26. 1; *15*. 1. 17; 1. 47. 1; 1. 52. pr.; *19*. 5. 10; *39*. 1. 23; 2. 7. 2; 2. 43. pr., 1/2; 3. 5; 3. 24. pr.; 3. 26; 5. 31. pr., 1, 3; 5. 32; 5. 35. pr., 1, 2; *41*. 1. 38; 1. 55; 1. 56. pr., 1; 1. 60; 2. 3. 17, 18; 2. 19. pr.; 2. 23. 2; 2. 40. 3; 2. 47; 3. 8. pr.; 3. 13. 1; 3. 21; 3. 33. 1; 3. 35; 4. 4. pr.; 4. 7. pr., 1, 2; 4. 8; 4. 10; 4. 13; 4. 14; 5. 2. 1; 6. 1. 2; 6. 5; 7. 8; 9. 3; *43*. 1. 4; 8. 4; 12. 4; 16. 19; 20. 4; 24. 18. 1; *44*. 4. 14; 4. 15.

[3] *D*. *12*. 6. 67. pr.; *22*. 3. 5. 1; *40*. 1. 20. 2, 3; 1. 23; 2. 22; 4. 9. pr.; 7. 14. pr., 1; 7. 15. 1; 7. 39. 1, 2, 4; 7. 40. pr., 1, 2, 3, 4, 5, 6, 7, 8; 8. 9; 9. 16. 3; 9. 21; 10. 2; 11. 3; 12. 38. pr., 1, 2, 3; 13. 4; 14. 5.

[4] D. *4*. 39; *9*. 2. 11. 5; 2. 51. pr.; 2. 52. 1, 2, 3, 4; 2. 55; 3. 5. 12 [two]; *11*. 3. 16; *42*. 8. 17. 1; 8. 19; 8. 21; *47*. 2. 48. 7; 2. 55 (54). 1; 2. 67 (66). 2, 3; 2. 73 (72); 2. 75 (74); 10. 20; 19. 6.

in which litigation about succession is (quantitatively) far overshadowed by, say, the negligence complex alone.

Secondly, the role of delict/quasi-delict is amazingly small: the 22 *responsa* here representing only 1·7 per cent of the total. Of those 22, seven are on the *lex Aquilia*, seven on *furtum*, three on *fraus creditorum* (which might plausibly have been put into the contract group), two on *effusa vel deiecta*, and one each on *iniuria*, *servi corruptio*, and the *actio de dolo*. There are none at all on *metus* or the *iudex qui litem suam fecerit*,[1] or on the praetorian delicts consisting in a breach of, or threat to, public peace and order.

Thirdly, while this last reflection is not germane to the problem of assessing the relative prominence of the civil jurisdictions, it may be noted that in a sense these various categories could be reduced to two great groups: the areas of potential difficulty more or less inseparable from normal family existence (succession, family law, property, status) and those resulting from voluntary extra relationships (contract plus delict); and that, if one looks at the *responsa* figures from this perspective, the preponderance of the former group is very striking, with more than three-quarters of the whole.[2] Again, an interesting contrast with the modern world is evident, though certainly not a surprising one: it is merely the litigious facet of Maine's aphorism about the movement of progressive societies from status to contract.[3]

It might be objected to all the foregoing, that even with so large a number as about 1,300 *responsa*, it could be that the mechanisms of compilation, or some other factor not now perceptible, produced results which—looked at from the perspective of someone trying to appraise the pattern of litigation—were accidentally odd or misleading. One way in which this possibility can be checked is to conduct a similar survey of the

[1] I had already concluded that the *actio quod metus causa* and that against the *iudex qui litem suam fecerit* must have been very rare in practice: *Roman Litigation*, pp. 116 f.

[2] This is broadly true notwithstanding that some of the 'property' cases may be rooted in contract, e.g. *usucapio*.

[3] *Ancient Law* (ed. Pollock), 174.

*rescripta* recorded in the Digest.[1] These undeniably reflect the queries of potential or actual litigants; and, unlike *responsa* (which are commonly preserved in clumps excerpted from books entitled *responsa* or *digesta*), the rescripts are scattered throughout the Digest in works of very different kinds. Although not as numerous as the *responsa*, they are still numerous enough to be worth analysing. In all I have counted 773 passages indicating a rescript; the great majority give the names of the emperors to whom they are credited, but some say merely something like '*saepe rescriptum est*'.

A much larger proportion of these, unfortunately, must be excluded from the 'private law' count than in the case of the *responsa*; not surprisingly, considering the unique, all-embracing authority from which they derive, the rescripts are very often concerned with points of public and criminal law, and also with statistically 'neutral' points of procedure—jurisdiction, appeals, etc. The figures attributable to those three excluded categories are: criminal law 167,[2] public law 137,[3] procedure

[1] Professor Kaser has suggested that a study of the Codex Iustinianus would have greatly increased the yield of *rescripta* available for analysis. This is certainly true; but the rescript material of the Codex is on the whole later than that of the Digest—i.e. so much the further distant from the Republic—and it seemed to me that the volume of material in the Digest was already big enough to allow fairly useful statistical estimates.

[2] D. *1*. 6. 2; 12. 1. 14; 15. 3. 2; 15. 4; 18. 14; 19. 3. 1, 2; *47*. 9. 4. 1; 9. 12. pr.; 11. 4; 12. 3. 4, 5, 7; 14. 1. pr.; 18. 1. pr.; 19. 3; 21. 2; 22. 1. pr., 2; *48*. 1. 12. 1; 2. 5; 2. 7. 2, 3, 4, 5; 2. 13; 2. 19. pr., 1; 2. 20; 2. 22; 3. 3; 3. 6. pr., 1; 3. 7; 3. 12. pr. [two]; 4. 5. 1, 2; 5. 6. 2; 5. 14 (13). 3, 8; 5. 28 (27). 6; 5. 33 (32). pr.; 5. 34 (33). pr.; 5. 39 (38). 5, 6, 8 [two], 10; 6. 5. 1; 6. 6; 8. 1. 3, 4, 5; 8. 4. 2; 8. 11. pr.; 8. 14; 9. 9. 2; 10. 1. 10; 10. 7; 10. 11; 10. 15. 3; 10. 29; 10. 31; 12. 3. pr., 1; 13. 6 (5); 15. 3. 1; 15. 6. pr., 1; 16. 7. pr.; 16. 14; 16. 16; 16. 18. pr., 1, 2; 17. 1. pr.; 17. 5. 2; 18. 1. 1, 2, 3, 4, 5, 6, 7, 10, 11, 12, 13, 14, 15, 16, 17, 19, 21, 22, 26; 18. 4; 18. 9. pr. [three], 2; 18. 10. pr.; 18. 12; 18. 15. 1, 2; 18. 16. pr., 1; 18. 17. 2; 18. 21; 19. 5. pr. [two]; 19. 8. 1, 12; 19. 9. 16; 19. 22; 19. 26; 19. 27. pr. [three]; 19. 28. 2, 6, 7, 14; 19. 30; 19. 31. 1; 19. 33; 19. 35; 19. 39; 19. 43. pr.; 20. 1. 3; 20. 2; 20. 6; 20. 7. 3, 4; 21. 3. 1, 2, 4, 5, 8; 22. 1; 22. 2; 22. 6. 2; 22. 7. 4, 10 [two], 18; 22. 16; 24. 2; *49*. 1. 1. 1; 1. 1. 3; 1. 4. 1; 1. 5. 3; 1. 8; 1. 9; 1. 10. 4; 1. 21. pr., 1, 3; 1. 5. 3; 9. 1; 11. 1; 13. 1. pr., 1; 14. 1. 2; 14. 23; 15. 25.

[3] D. *1*. 8. 4. pr.; 8. 6. 1; 8. 7; 16. 4. pr., 5; 16. 10. 1; 18. 8; 18. 9; 18. 13. 1; *2*. 12. 9; 14. 37; *3*. 2. 2. 2; *11*. 7. 6. 1; 7. 12. pr.; 7. 37. 1; *39*. 4. 6; 4. 7. pr., 1; 4. 16. pr., 2, 4, 6, 9, 10, 11, 12, 14; *47*. 10. 13. 7; *49*. 14. 2. 1, 2, 4, 5, 7; 14. 3. 4, 5 [two], 6, 8, 9; 14. 6. pr.; 14. 7; 14. 8; 14. 12; 14. 13. 4; 14. 13. 10; 14. 15. 2; 14. 22. pr.; 14. 26; 14. 30; 14. 31; 14. 32; 14. 34; 15. 9; 15. 25; 16. 4. pr., 5, 9; 16. 5. 6, 8; 16. 6. 7; 16. 19. 2; 18. 4. pr., 1; 18. 5. pr.; *50*. 1. 8; 1. 11. pr.; 1. 18; 1. 24;

55:[1] total 359, which, when subtracted from the whole body, leaves 414 for analysis: less than a third of the number of usable *responsa*, but a figure still big enough to give statistically interesting results.

Dividing these 414 rescripts on the same principle as before the result is as follows:

| | |
|---|---|
| Succession | 257[2] |
| Family law | 74[3] |

1. 37. pr., 2; 1. 38. pr., 1, 2, 3, 4, 5, 6; 2. 13. pr., 1, 2, 3; 2. 14; 4. 6. pr., 1; 4. 7. 1; 4. 11. 1, 2, 3, 4; 4. 14. 4, 6; 4. 18. 30; 6. 3 (2–1); 6. 6 (5). 2, 5, 6, 9, 10, 13; 7. 5 (4). pr., 1, 3, 5; 7. 7 (6); 8. 11 (9). pr., 1, 2; 8. 12 (9–3). pr., 1 (4), 2 (5), 3 (6), 4. (7), 5 (8), 6 (9); 8. 13 (9–10); 9. 5; 10. 5. pr.; 10. 6; 10. 7. pr.; 12. 1. pr., 5, 6; 12. 6. 1, 2, 3; 12. 7; 12. 8; 12. 9; 12. 12. pr., 1; 12. 13. pr., 1; 12. 15; 15. 3. 1; 15. 4. 10.

[1] D. *2*. 1. 11. pr.; 4. 3; 8. 7. pr.; *3*. 1. 8 [two]; 1. 11; 2. 24; 3. 33. 2; *4*. 6. 26. 9; 8. 27. 2; *5*. 1. 2. 3, 4 [two]; 1. 36. pr.; 1. 47; *11*. 2. 2; *12*. 3. 4. pr. [three]; 3. 10; *22*. 3. 13; 3. 29. pr.; 5. 3. 1, 2, 3, 4, 6; *42*. 1. 15. pr., 1, 3, 8, 9; 1. 31; 1. 33; 1. 35; 1. 59. 1; 1. 63; 4. 7. 16; 7. 4; *44*. 3. 9; *49*. 14. 3. 1; 14. 18. 4, 8, 10; 14. 22. 1, 2, 3; 14. 27; 14. 29. 2; *50*. 13. 1. 9, 10, 12; 13. 2; 17. 28; 17. 101.

[2] D. *2*. 14. 16. pr.; 14. 52. 3; 15. 3. pr.; 15. 7. 2; *4*. 2. 18; 4. 7. 9, 10; 4. 22; *5*. 1. 50. 2; 1. 51; 2. 7; 2. 8. 2; 2. 8. 16; 2. 30. 1; 3. 5. pr., 1; 3. 7. pr., 1, 2; 3. 43; *7*. 5. 12; *10*. 2. 18. 3; 2. 20. 1; 7. 14. 7, 14; *12*. 6. 2. 1; 6. 3; 6. 4; 6. 5; *22*. 1. 17. 2; 6. 9. 5; *26*. 4. 1. 3; *28*. 1. 15; 1. 20. 9; 3. 6. 6; 3. 12. pr.; 4. 3. 1; 5. 1. pr., 5, 6; 5. 9. 2; 5. 30; 5. 52 (51). pr.; 6. 2. 4; 6. 10. 6; 7. 18. pr.; *29*. 1. 3; 1. 9. 1; 1. 13. 4; 1. 15. 2; 1. 24; 1. 28; 1. 30; 1. 34. pr.; 1. 41. 1; 1. 44; 2. 6. 3; 2. 12; 2. 25. 2, 3; 2. 30. pr.; 2. 52. pr.; 4. 2. pr.; 4. 10. 1; 5. 1. 5; 5. 1. 28/29; 5. 2; 5. 15. 1; 7. 1; 7. 6. pr.; *30*. 34. 3; 37. pr.; 41. 3; 41. 7; 73. 1; 74; 77; 111; 112. pr., 4; 113. 1; 114. 11, 12, 14, 15; *31*. 8. 5; 61. 1; 64; 67. 10; 70. pr.; *32*. 1. 9; 8. 2; 11. 2, 18, 19, 23, 24, 25; 58; 96; *33*. 1. 23; 1. 24; 2. 23; 5. 1; 8. 6. 4; 8. 8. 7; *34*. 1. 2. pr.; 1. 3 [two]; 1. 14. 1; 3. 9; 3. 25; 4. 13; 5. 16 (17). pr.; 6. 2; 8. 3. pr.; 9. 1; 9. 2. 1; 9. 5. 1, 9; 9. 6; *35*. 1. 33. 2; 1. 72. 3; 1. 77. pr.; 1. 90; 1. 92; 1. 113; 2. 49. pr.; 2. 59. 1; 2. 89. pr., 1; 3. 3. 4, 5; 3. 6; *36*. 1. 1. 17; 1. 3. 4; 1. 11. 2 [two]; 1. 12; 1. 15. 2, 4; 1. 17 (16). 17; 1. 18 (17). 8 [two]; 1. 25 (24); 1. 30 (29); 1. 31 (30). 5; 1. 32 (31). 1; 1. 57 (55). 1; 1. 60 (58). 3; 1. 65 (63). 5; 3. 1. 11; 3. 5. 1, 3 [two]; 3. 14. 1; 4. 1. 3; 4. 3. 1, 3; 4. 5. 16/18; *37*. 5. 5. 6; 6. 1. 14, 21; 6. 5, pr.; 7. 1. pr.; 7. 9; 8. 3; 8. 4; 9. 1. 14; 9. 8; 10. 1. 5; 10. 3. 1, 5; 12. 1. 4; 14. 3; 14. 4; 14. 5. 1; 14. 8. pr.; 14. 17. pr.; 14. 23. 1; 15. 4; *38*. 1. 7. 4; 2. 3. pr.; 2. 16. 4; 2. 22; 16. 1. 1 [two]; 16. 2. 7; 16. 3. 12; 17. 1. 3; 17. 2. 29/32; 17. 2. 47; *40*. 4. 26; 4. 46; 4. 56; 5. 12. pr., 2; 5. 24. 5, 6, 9, 21 [two]; 5. 26. 2, 3/4, 8; 5. 30. pr., 3, 5, 6, 7, 13, 15, 16, 17; 5. 31. 1, 4; 5. 37; 5. 46. 3; 5. 51. 9; *42*. 4. 7. 19; 6. 1. 3, 6; *47*. 4. 1. 7; *49*. 1. 5. 1, 2; 1. 14. 1; 14. 13. 6; 14. 43; 14. 48. pr.; 14. 49; 17. 13; *50*. 16. 220. 2.

[3] D. *1*. 7. 21; 7. 32. 1; 7. 39; *4*. 4. 11. 2; 4. 45. 1; *5*. 1. 2. 3; *15*. 1. 52. pr.; *23*. 2. 20; 2. 45. pr.; 2. 57a; 2. 58; 3. 9. 3; 3. 33; 3. 40; 4. 11; *24*. 1. 7. 5, 6; 2. 11. 2; 3. 2. 2; *25*. 3. 1. 15; 3. 5. 6, 7, 9, 11, 14, 17; 4. 1 pr.; *26*. 1. 3. 1; 5. 2; 5. 12. 1; 5. 13. pr.; 5. 18; 5. 29; *26*. 7. 2. pr. [two]; 7. 3. 4; 7. 7. 14; 7. 11; 7. 12. 1; 7. 33. 1; 8. 1. pr.; 8. 5. pr., 3; 10. 1. 4, 7; 10. 3. pr., 13; *27*. 1. 5; 1. 6. 6; 1. 7; 1. 10. 8; 1. 12. pr.; 1. 15. 16; 1. 17. 1, 4, 6; 1. 26; 1. 44. pr.; 2. 1. 1; 3. 1. 15 [two]; 3. 17; 5. 1. 2; 8. 1. 2, 8, 9; 8. 6; 8. 9; 9. 2; 9. 13. pr., 10. 1. 1; 10. 16. pr.; *43*. 30. 1. 3.

| | |
|---|---|
| Contract | 48[1] |
| Status | 14[2] |
| Property | 12[3] |
| Delict | 9[4] |

The graph-profile, so to speak, of this distribution is in some ways rather different from that of the *responsa*—the emperors were, for instance, evidently consulted relatively much more often than were the jurists in matters of family law, especially *tutela*, relatively less often in matters of contract and property—but the very same conspicuous over-all features are apparent. Sixty-two per cent, roughly the same proportion as with the *responsa*, of the total are cases involving problems of succession: a large over-all majority. At the other end of the scale, only 2·1 per cent—again much the same proportion as with the *responsa*—involve problems of delict. And, in general, the preponderance of family- and status-centred cases over contract and delict is once again huge. The result of comparing the two sets of figures is to confirm, firstly, that the *responsa* do indeed represent (as was assumed at the outset) a mass of material derived like the rescripts from actual practice; secondly, that the statistical pattern of that real practice can be discerned in crude outline from the conspicuous features of the distribution of *responsa* and *rescripta*.[5]

[1] D. *2.* 14. 8; 14. 10. pr.; 14. 60; *3.* 5. 3. 4; 5. 5. 14 (12); *4.* 1. 7 pr.; 4. 18. 3; 4. 20. 1; *12.* 2. 5. 1; 2. 13. 6; 6. 23. 1; 6. 26. pr.; 6. 39; *13.* 6. 3. pr.; 7. 13. pr.; 7. 17; 7. 26. pr.; *14.* 6. 15; *16.* 1. 2. 3 [two]; 1. 4. pr.; 3. 7. 3; *17.* 1. 6. 7; 1. 8. 8; 1. 12. 10; 2. 52. 5; *18.* 1. 42; 1. 71; 2. 16; 3. 4. pr.; *19.* 1. 43; 2. 9. 1, 4; 2. 15. 3, 5 [two], 6; 2. 19. 9; *20.* 1. 16. 9; 3. 1. 2; 5. 12. pr.; *22.* 1. 17. pr., 1, 3; 1. 32. pr.; *39.* 5. 12; *42.* 5. 30; *46.* 3. 5. 2.

[2] D. *1.* 5. 8; 5. 18; *40.* 1. 8. 2, 3; 2. 9. 1; 7. 34. 1; 8. 1; 8. 3; 9. 11. 1; 9. 15. pr.; 10. 6; 12. 27. pr./1; 12. 43; 15. 4.

[3] D. *5.* 1. 37; *6.* 2. 11. pr.; 2. 12. pr.; *8.* 2. 14; 3. 16; 3. 17; 3. 35; 4. 2; *10.* 1. 7; *11.* 4. 3; 4. 5; *43.* 24. 15. 6.

[4] D. *4.* 2. 9. 3; 2. 16. 2; 4. 11. pr.; 8. 32. 14; *9.* 2. 29. 1; *42.* 8. 7; 8. 10. 1; *47.* 10. 40; 12. 3. 3.

[5] Professor Kaser has privately suggested that the *responsa* and *rescripta* are collectively not necessarily a guide to the relative frequency of *litigation* in one field or another, as it is possible that—precisely on foot of a *responsum* or a *rescriptum*—the parties might have settled out of court. I admit the likelihood of this. But it seems to me a factor common to all areas of potential litigation; and since what is interesting is not the absolute but the relative frequencies, this common factor can be disregarded as likely to have 'cancelled itself out' as between different

Besides the *responsa* and *rescripta*, there are some cases presented in the Digest which, from circumstantial indications, can be seen to have been real. These represent a much more difficult body of evidence for the present purpose, firstly, because the criteria for spotting a 'real' case not signalized by *respondere* or *rescribere* are naturally debatable; secondly, because the number of such cases identifiable as real beyond reasonable doubt is very small, perhaps too small for statistical exploitation. None the less it will do no harm to look at them to see whether, in general, they do or do not accord with the pattern jointly suggested by the *responsa* and *rescripta*. Of the eighty-one cases counted, the large majority are identified as real because they are presented as the subject of imperial *decreta*, i.e. judgments in actual litigation; the rest are included on criteria which their context makes obvious.

Among these 81 cases, 5 concern criminal law;[1] the remaining 76, arranged according to the scheme adopted for *responsa* and *rescripta*, are distributed as follows:

| | |
|---|---|
| Succession | 52[2] |
| Contract | 11[3] |
| Family law | 7[4] |
| Property | 4[5] |
| Delict | 2[6] |
| Status | 1[7] |

areas. If one assumes that half of all cases on which a *responsum* or *rescriptum* was sought were settled or not proceeded with, this still leaves the relative frequencies unchanged—in the absence, that is, of a factor (unknown to me but in theory absolutely possible) which would make settlement more likely in one area than in another.

[1] D. *47*. 18. 1. 2; *48*. 7. 7; 10. 1. 4; 13. 12 (10). 1; 18. 17. pr.

[2] D. *5*. 2. 28; *19*. 1. 13. 5; *22*. 1. 3. pr., 3; 3. 26; *23*. 4. 30; *28*. 3. 3. 2; 4. 3. pr.; 5. 19; 5. 42 (41); 5. 93 (92); *29*. 2. 97; *30*. 49. pr.; *31*. 29. pr.; 57; *32*. 11. 1; 27. pr., 1, 2; 78. 6; *34*. 1. 14. 3; 5. 9 (10). 1; 9. 3; 9. 5. 10, 15; 9. 12; 9. 16. 1, 2; 9. 18. pr.; *35*. 1. 48; 1. 50; 2. 1. 14; 2. 11. 2; 3. 7; 3. 8; *36*. 1. 1. 12; 1. 18 (17). pr.; 1. 19. (18). 3; 1. 23 (22). pr.; 1. 36 (35); 1. 38 (37). 1; 1. 52 (50); 1. 56 (54); 1. 76 (74). pr., 1; 1. 83 (81); *37*. 14. 24; *38*. 17. 2. 9; *49*. 1. 14. pr.; 14. 47. pr.

[3] D. *4*. 3. 1; 4. 18. 1, 2, 3; 4. 38; *14*. 2. 9; 3. 13. pr.; *17*. 2. 25; *22*. 1. 6. pr., 1; 1. 16.

[4] D. *23*. 2. 29; *26*. 5. 28; 7. 7. 4; 7. 53; *27*. 3. 1. 3; *37*. 14. 7. pr.; *43*. 30. 3. 5.

[5] D. *7*. 8. 22. pr.; *8*. 4. 13; 5. 8. 5; 5. 17. 1.

[6] D. *11*. 6. 7. 3; 47. 2. 52. 20.

[7] D. *40*. 12. 23. 2.

Even in this very much smaller sample, the main characteristics observed in *responsa* and *rescripta* recur: over-all majority (in this case over 68 per cent) from the field of succession; tiny role of delict (2·6 per cent); very heavy preponderance of family- and status-centred problems.

I hope therefore that whatever weaknesses of method may be found in the details of my crude enumeration of *responsa, rescripta,* and real cases otherwise signalized—and whatever further work remains to be done on the Digest as evidence for actual litigious patterns[1]—these three observations may be admitted as valid pointers to the relative prominence in litigation of different legal areas, not only in the period of classical jurisprudence, but (for reasons explained at the beginning of this chapter) in the Republic also.[2]

It remains to relate these pointers to my attempt to describe the pattern of the Republican judicature.

Firstly, as to the huge preponderance of family- and status-centred litigation, including succession cases. It will be seen in the next chapter,[3] firstly, that all litigation was painful and

[1] There is no doubt, it seems to me, that the Digest alone offers immense scope for further analysis in regard to the realities of litigation. Professor Kaser suggested, in connection with my conclusions about the predominance of succession cases, that my own analysis might have been brought to the point of distinguishing different types of succession litigation—*hereditatis petitio, querela inofficiosi testamenti,* fideicommissary cases, legacies, etc. The difficulty here, however, is that a very large proportion of what may broadly be called 'succession' cases—e.g. questions regarding the interpretation of phrases—would be impossible to assign with confidence to one field rather than another. It is for this reason that I do not equate all succession cases with centumviral cases; obviously the vindication of a legacy might have been done before an *unus iudex*; but on the other hand, the mere fact that a text ostensibly shows a *responsum* on how a purported legacy is to be interpreted does not mean that the litigation which called forth the *responsum* was not centumviral, since the disposition of legacies might easily be a component of the *querela inofficiosi testamenti,* for which centumviral jurisdiction is clearly established.

[2] It is true that several objections can be made to the use of this material as evidence for the Republic. For example, many 'succession' cases in the Digest concern *fideicommissa,* which were not enforced in the Republic. But it may be presumed that in an era which did not enforce *fideicommissa,* the object of a *fideicommissum* would sometimes have been achieved by direct testamentary disposition.

[3] The chapter-sequence is certainly unfortunate at this point, where it would have been well to have had the material on the painfulness of litigation already presented. But I wished to bring the Roman sensitivity about litigation into the closest possible association with the *iudicium privatum* and the *unus iudex* (dealt with in the final chapter).

embarrassing to the Roman; secondly, that some kinds of litigation were especially so. While of course the kind of action which (if one defended it unsuccessfully) carried formal *infamia* must have been the most painful of all, at any rate for the defendant, still the texts suggest a strongly marked fastidious reluctance to have one's affairs booted about in a public law-court with the attendant risk of being cruelly abused in public by one's adversary's counsel. It seems to me as good as certain that, high up in the 'especially painful' category of cases, were those the litigation of which involved exploring family relations. The businessman pursuing a debt, or being himself pursued by a creditor, might be thick-skinned enough to put up with vituperation about his business morals; it would be a different matter if he had to let the world see his squabbles with his wife or his brother or in general what went on within the walls of his house. When this general reflection is placed alongside the plain fact that succession cases were commoner than all others put together, the superficial conclusion might be that either of these observations, if true, must tend to invalidate the other. In my belief a quite different conclusion is to be drawn: namely, that considerations of embarrassment actually must have *depressed* the number of succession cases reaching the point of litigation, so that, if the embarrassment or loss-of-face factor had been absent, we would see an even more gigantic preponderance of succession cases and of the family- and status-centred group generally.[1] It is true that we might also see more cases brought e.g. on *iniuria*, but the same huge relative discrepancy would certainly exist between the fields of succession and delict. Accordingly, the huge role of succession in the litigation pattern should be viewed against the background of certainty that very many succession disputes were quietly settled by agreement or informal arbitration.

The principal importance here of these observations on suc-

[1] Of course it is true that inheritances and legacies might be left to 'outsiders', not members of the family in any sense. But since no doubt the normal case of testamentary succession (and all cases of intestate succession) involved persons near to the deceased in the family sense, I would think it permissible to include succession cases within the broad category of family- and status-centred litigation.

cession lies in their bearing on the *centumviri*. The succession cases, as counted by me, include cases on legacies and *fideicommissa*, and these were not litigated before *centumviri* unless they arose peripherally in actions about the validity of a will or the entitlement to an inheritance; so that I certainly do not say that the quantitative role of the *centumviri* can be simply read off my 'succession' figures. But equally it would be quite wrong to restrict the *centumviri*'s allotment merely to *responsa*, etc., expressly about the *querela inofficiosi testamenti* or the interpretation of wills, because other questions, e.g. about legacies or manumissions or *donationes mortis causa*, must have arisen as incidental questions in the hearing of a *querela* and thus been within the centumviral purview (*fideicommissa* too, though since these were enforced only from the time of Augustus they are not relevant to calculations about the Republic). Accordingly, while it is hopeless to attempt to quantify exactly the share of litigation discharged by the *centumviri*, I feel it is safe to call it probable that a large share of the (roughly) three-fifths of all litigation representing succession problems came potentially within their domain; and this means that they were in practical importance and quantitative prominence anything but the marginal phenomenon which they are seen as in the textbooks. This conclusion, moreover, harmonizes well with, e.g., the evidence of Pliny, from whom one would scarcely suspect the existence of any jurisdiction other than that of the *centumviri*.[1]

If we look now at the fields where the *recuperatores* are agreed to have been active, a very different conclusion must be reached. Quite a number of the cases on free/unfree status are expressly referred to the *liberalis causa*, and obviously many others may have arisen in that setting without our being told so. But even if the entire bloc of free/unfree status cases is assigned to the *recuperatores*, and even if we add an indefinite but good number of the manumission-on-succession cases (which I included in the 'succession' category) and then add the (very tiny) number of cases on what Schmidlin calls the 'gemeingefährliche Delikte' plus some share of the procedural cases originally excluded

[1] See above, pp. 35 ff.

(some of them must have arisen in circumstances where *recuperatores* were used to enforce the praetorian authority), we still arrive at a proportion of all litigation which is not even roughly quantifiable, but which can fairly be called very small; on the assumptions most favourable to frequent recuperatorial activity, still less (I would think) than a tenth of the whole.

If one now eliminates both centumviral and recuperatorial material one is left with the area of the *unus iudex*. The proportion of the burden of all litigation normally falling on him cannot be accurately quantified any more than in the case of the other two jurisdictions; but my impression would be that, if one excludes the large slice represented by *centumviri* and the very much smaller slice represented by *recuperatores*, one arrives at the very crude guess that he accounted for about half of all litigation, perhaps a little more. It was a very special half, and the very special features qualifying a case for treatment by the *unus iudex* will be examined in the final chapter, once an important but subtle dimension—the Roman distaste for litigation—has been added to the general picture.

# IV

# 'Loss of Face' as a Factor Inhibiting Litigation

AFTER assessing the rough statistical pattern of litigation as a step towards elucidating the structure and mutual relations of the parts of the Roman judicature, the next step might well be to form some idea of how litigation, as an incident of life, was looked on by the Romans. Naturally it would be an easy guess that they, like people in the modern world, disliked lawsuits in general; but there were some peculiar dimensions of Roman litigious practice, and their evaluation may help towards a more subtle, more differentiated conclusion than merely that all litigation was unwelcome.

It is a commonplace that the Romans, like some other nations in early history, were extremely sensitive on the score of personal reputation (*existimatio*),[1] and it would be interesting to see if the Roman sources provide information on the bearing of litigation on *existimatio*. In order to give this inquiry a comparative perspective, however, it may be worth mentioning an institution of early Irish law[2] in which this question is specifically dealt with.

This institution is found in a legal tract entitled *Cóic conara fugill* ('The five ways to judgment').[3] According to the text, certain breaches of the law of procedure were subject to a fixed

[1] See the examples given in D. 47. 10 (*de iniuriis et famosis libellis*) of the slights and insults which could ground an *actio iniuriarum*.

[2] The text of the earliest surviving Irish law tracts belongs to about the seventh century A.D., but this is merely the written version of far more ancient material. See Binchy, 'Ancient Irish Law', 1 *Irish Jurist* (1966) 87 ff.

[3] Text translated (into German) and with commentary by Rudolf v. Thurneysen, in 7 *Abhandlungen der preussischen Akademie der Wissenschaften* (Phil.-hist. Klasse) (1925).

fine, namely one cow; for instance, the failure to adopt the correct 'way' before the beginning of the hearing, or the departure from one 'way' to another after the beginning of the hearing, or the use of too loud or too inaudible a voice during the hearing; but also—and here lies the relevance of the text in the present context—behaviour which the Irish called *anfine n-ae*, literally, 'storminess of advocacy'. In this instance there was a special rule, explained by Thurneysen[1] as follows:

It was immemorial practice for the parties to a law-suit to heap the maximum abuse on one another. However, liability to the special action for insult could be avoided by the fixed payment of one cow, which was much less than the normal compositions for an insult, which frequently amounted to the full 'honour price'[2] of the person insulted. The text allows this rule to apply only where the parties have agreed on this standard composition beforehand, and where the party insulted claims the composition while the case is still going on, before the judge gives his decision. If these conditions are not fulfilled, the law treats abuse as falling into two categories. If it consists merely of an attack on the style of the other party's pleading, then it is not actionable at all once the judge has pronounced judgment. But if it is abuse of a grosser kind,[3] then the party so reviled can recover damages afterwards of the same amount as if the abuse had been uttered altogether outside the context of the law-suit.

That is, the party uttering the insults cannot avail himself of the advantageous provision limiting his liability to the relatively modest value of one cow.

Three points of importance result from these curious provisions: first, abusing one's opponent was a normal feature of litigation; secondly, this abuse did not fall under the ordinary law relating to insult, but was in a sense 'privileged'; thirdly, this 'privilege' did not make it any the less painful for the person abused. Once he let himself in for a lawsuit, he had to put up with abuse, or at any rate accept a relatively small composition as amends for it; unless, in default of prior agreement

[1] At p. 62. [2] 'Eneclann'.

[3] The text mentions the eight deadly insults: these are allegations of cuckoldry, bastardy, epilepsy, leprosy, impotence, blindness, deafness, or lameness.

and in a case of gross abuse, he had the opportunity of suing as though for an extra-procedural insult.

If we now turn back to the Roman world, we shall naturally not expect to find exact parallels to the early Irish law, but it will be of some interest to inquire in what way Roman law faced up to the same range of problems. A good starting-point might be to observe that the Roman law both of the Republic and of the classical period did contain a concept which connected litigation and reputation with one another, viz. the so-called *infamia* or *ignominia*, the degradation associated with condemnation in certain types of action. Viewed as a material consequence, this degradation meant that the person concerned was excluded from certain legal operations which were honourable in the Roman eye; according to Gaius[1] the praetor would refuse to allow him to represent another, or to be represented by another, in litigation. This kind of *infamia* is in modern usage called 'praetorian' in order to distinguish it from 'censorial' *infamia*; the latter describes merely the inherent right of the censors to place a mark of disgrace (*nota*) against the name of a citizen guilty of immoral conduct, and, unlike 'praetorian' *infamia*, it had no necessary association with condemnation in an action, nor had it any specific consequences in the field of procedure.

The word *infamia* in the praetorian sense was not a technical term; neither was the word *ignominia*, sometimes used in this context but more properly belonging to the sphere of criminal or public law. Gaius himself expressly says[2] that the edict nowhere describes a person as *ignominiosus*; it was merely conventional to use this word of someone to whom representation in litigation has been denied because of condemnation in certain actions. In the Digest title on the subject, which bears the rubric *De his qui notantur infamia*, the words *infamia notatur* are agreed to be a Justinianic interpolation.[3] This 'praetorian *infamia*', then, is merely an untechnical expression, based on colloquial usage, and intended to sum up the various prohibitions imposed by the praetor, and, as Kaser has written,[4]

[1] *Inst.* 4. 182. [2] Ibid. [3] Kaser, 73 *ZSS* (1956) 245. [4] Op. cit. 233.

it was the late classical jurists who first used the word *infamia* in a more or less settled sense to denote the different conditions of legally relevant disgrace; before that time, the word meant no more than the loss of respect in society, and belonged to the extra-legal sphere. The sources in the Republic and early Principate use *infamia* to mean simply 'a bad name' or 'to get a bad name', 'to be ill thought of'; thus Gellius, for instance, cites the statement of C. Caesar as *pontifex maximus* that *patroni* cannot let down their clients *sine summa infamia*,[1] and what is meant here is not some legally significant form of disgrace, but merely that the behaviour in question is shameful according to general notions and exposes the faithless *patronus* to public contempt.

The Romans, sensitive as they were about their reputations, felt the loss of public esteem very keenly; how keenly, may be seen from many passages in their literature. We find for example in Cicero's speeches—particularly in the *pro Quinctio*—the notion that honour and good name are almost more important than life itself, and, even making allowances for the fact that this idea (familiar also in modern European literature) is a commonplace of rhetoric with the Romans—as the manuals of rhetoric composed by Cicero and Quintilian reveal[2]—still the exaggeration must rest on a basis of some truth. Fear of the loss of honour, *metus infamiae*, must therefore have sorely preoccupied anyone threatened with a lawsuit in which condemnation would involve praetorian sanctions commonly interpreted as disgrace. And in fact we find in the *Institutes* of Justinian[3] (which in this respect quite likely go back to Gaius) that *metus infamiae*, the fear of public disgrace, is one of the things said to inhibit *temeritas litigantium* (rashness in litigating), whether on the side of the defendant or even of the plaintiff. If this factor is related to a concrete legal situation, e.g. of *societas* (a contract to which an 'infaming' action was attached, the *actio pro socio*), it suggests that a partner who is having difficulties with the other partner or partners will go to considerable lengths to prevent the institution of the *actio pro socio*, whether by giving

[1] *N.A.* 5. 13. 6.
[2] e.g. Cic. *De orat.* 2. 172; Quint. *Inst. or.* 6. 2. 23.
[3] 4.16. pr.

in to the demands made on him, or by settling on a compromise basis.

It seems clear, at any rate, that the possibility of incurring *infamia* operated as a factor strongly inhibiting litigation. But the further question arises whether (as in the early Irish law) factors falling short of *infamia* may have had a similarly inhibiting effect. There is the possibility—given the Roman sensitiveness about *existimatio*—that *existimatio* might be threatened even in a case where no question of praetorian *infamia* was involved.

It is worth noting here that the general Roman view of litigation was unfavourable. This would be true of modern society as well; but the Roman distaste for it must seem to us exaggerated. We find, for example, Nepos saying of Atticus in his biography of Cicero's friend that he *in ius de sua re numquam iit, iudicium nullum habuit*;[1] this occurs in the midst of a litany of Atticus' many virtues. Even though in modern society litigation is unpopular, it is doubtful whether a biographer or obituarist would think it worth saying, as a mark of his subject's virtue, that he never instituted a lawsuit concerning his own affairs, and that he was never sued by anyone else. And if we turn to Cicero's correspondence with Atticus, we find several indications that bringing a dispute as far as the court was something to be avoided like the plague; Atticus is for example asked[2] to make sure that debts are paid, or that some other difference be settled, without any 'fuss' (*scrupulus*). It is true that the most unequivocal of these passages refers to the possibility of an *actio pro socio* between two brothers, a lawsuit painful in itself but also containing the possibility of *infamia*; but in the other passages too one can detect a general desire to avoid litigation. In addition, Cicero at one point makes this explicit: in his *De officiis*[3] he admonishes the reader to be generous in all legal relationships, and indeed to be ready to yield, if necessary, even

[1] *Atticus* 6. 3.

[2] *Ad Att.* 2. 4. 1. Cicero says: *Cura ut cum Titinio quoquo modo transigas. Si in eo quod ostenderat non stat, mihi maxime placet ea quae male empta sunt reddi, si voluntate Pomponiae fieri poterit; si ne id quidem, nummi potius reddantur quam ullus sit scrupulus.*

[3] 2. 64.

something to which he may be well entitled: but above all to stay clear of lawsuits: *a litibus . . . quantum liceat et nescio an paulo plus etiam, quam liceat* [*abhorrere*]—even if this modesty might be criticized as insufficient firmness in standing on one's own rights.

These passages reveal a notion of personal dignity certainly connected with class, and which might be paralleled in the upper strata of other societies. It is consistent with the dignity—and so with the *existimatio*—of the upper-class Roman to keep clear of all squabbles; to settle business differences so far as possible while keeping them among the parties immediately involved, and to shield, so far as possible, one's affairs from public exposure. It is to this ideal that Seneca's complaint[1] about Tiberius' behaviour should be referred: when he was petitioned for money in order to allow the petitioners to pay off creditors who had lent them money, he forced them to explain publicly to the Senate how it had come about that they found it necessary to borrow the money in the first place. Seneca describes this experience, from the point of view of the petitioners, as *ignominia*, because it obliged them to divulge their private affairs to strangers.

Merely to be involved in a lawsuit, then, must have been mortifying for a reputable Roman. But Roman litigation contained a peculiar feature, absent from modern litigation as a rule, which made this mortification far more acute; acute to the point of bringing one's *existimatio* into jeopardy. This feature was the conventional form taken by Roman forensic rhetoric. Just as with the early Irish, the *existimatio* of the Roman litigant was exposed, in a public hearing, to the most cruel attacks. Proof of this is present in abundance, not only in the actually surviving court speeches of Cicero, but also in a mass of instructional literature on rhetoric. The advocate in a Roman action was permitted to use the most unbridled language about his client's adversary, or even his friends or relations or witnesses; and this was so even where the expressions used were quite irrelevant to the issue at trial; indeed, the less relevant the attack, the more extreme it might be. What the Romans

[1] *De beneficiis* 2. 8. 2.

called *reprehensio vitae* or *vituperatio*—a personal attack on the character of one's opponent—was taken as absolutely normal;[1] and rhetoric manuals dealt in great detail with the most effective way to construct a *vituperatio*. Cicero twice[2] actually uses a triad, in pointing out what must be done to one's client's adversary, which is strikingly similar to the modern English notion of actionable defamation: he must be brought into *odium*, *invidia*, and *contemptio*.

It may be noted incidentally that *vituperatio* was in no way confined to criminal or sensitive political cases, but was the rule also in ordinary civil cases as well. Thus in Cicero's *pro Quinctio* what is in issue is whether the adversary of Cicero's client, Sextus Naevius, had taken possession of Quinctius' property in conformity with the provisions of the edict: a purely civil dispute. Cicero calls Naevius at various points a clown,[3] an ill-bred grabber,[4] untrustworthy,[5] treacherous,[6] impious,[7] violent,[8] avaricious,[9] vindictive,[10] shameless,[11] the author of an unparalleled dirty trick;[12] all this abuse being combined with incessant hostile irony. In his *pro Roscio Comoedo* Cicero's attack on Fannius Chaerea is even worse; not even his personal appearance is spared: his face is represented as proof that he is made up of lies and fraud;[13] the pimp in Plautus' comedy *Pseudolus* is said to be Fannius' model on account of his disgusting mode of life;[14] Fannius is also a shameless and greedy perjurer.[15] In the *pro Caecina* Cicero's client's opponent, Sextus Aebutius, comes in for similar insults: he is a shameless swindler and rogue, while simultaneously a fool;[16] a man who turned his back on law, morals, and duty in order to devote himself to violence, including murder.[17] Further examples could be added;[18] but it is clear that this kind of advocacy was taken for

[1] In *pro Murena* 11 Cicero calls the *reprehensio vitae* a sort of formality expected of a prosecutor: *lex quaedam accusatoria*.

[2] *Rhet. ad Her.* 1. 8; *De inventione* 1. 22.

[3] *Pro Quinctio* 11.

[4] Ibid.

[5] Ibid. 14.

[6] Ibid. 26, 46, 56.

[7] Ibid. 26.

[8] Ibid. 5, 30.

[9] Ibid. 9, 12, 21, 38.

[10] Ibid. 46, 48.

[11] Ibid. 53, 56.

[12] Ibid. 22, 79.

[13] *Pro. Rosc. Com.* 20.

[14] Ibid.

[15] Ibid. 4 and *passim*.

[16] *Pro Caecina* 14, 23.

[17] Ibid. 93.

[18] e.g. the case about an alleged debt heard by Gellius (*N.A.* 14. 2) in which evidence was given, or at any rate it was said, that the defendant was a person of

granted, and was practised in a degree quite unknown today. Its relevance in the present context is clear; quite apart from the general disinclination to litigate, we must understand that anyone concerned for his *existimatio*—as Kaser puts it, his 'unangetastete Ehrenstellung'—would be extremely slow to litigate, even if he thought himself entirely in the right, if litigation obliged him to submit to this kind of attack.

This Roman convention of rhetorical abuse presents an amazing contrast with the notions of personal honour on which the delictal forms of *iniuria* are based. The sources on *iniuria* suggest that the slightest, most indirect affront might ground an *actio iniuriarum*, e.g. the demand for payment of a debt made to a surety before first being made to the principal debtor (thus implying the latter's insolvency).[1] Verbal insult as the basis of an *actio iniuriarum* may at first have been confined to *convicium*, i.e. to abuse uttered by a crowd specially gathered for the purpose, and it is certainly rather surprising that the Digest title on *iniuria* says little about insults perpetrated by an individual; but it may be assumed that this could in fact ground the *actio*, particularly if the insult were public; we have for instance the testimony of the *Rhetorica ad Herennium*[2] that in two different cases actors were sued because they had insulted individuals from the stage. But rhetorical abuse in court was apparently excepted; complete freedom prevailed, and there is not the slightest suggestion in the sources that advocates were in any danger of being sued on account of the expressions they used. Schulz does indeed say[3] that the phrase often found in Cicero's speeches *quem honoris causa nomino*, used of someone to whom one had to refer in the course of one's speech, shows that merely to mention an uninvolved third party in the course of litigation might bring down on one an action for *iniuria* (unless one used this formula for saving the other's face); but there is no evidence

bad reputation; this had nothing to do with the point at issue, and was evidently the result of the plaintiff's counsel practising what he had learned about court rhetoric and *reprehensio vitae* of one's opponent: *illum autem unde petebatur hominem esse non bonae rei vitaque turpi et sordida convictumque volgo in mendaciis plenumque esse perfidiarum et fraudum ostendebatur.*

[1] Gaius, D. 47. 10. 19. [2] 2. 13. 19. [3] *Classical Roman Law*, 1016.

whatever for this assertion. On the contrary, it seems to have been the case that the Roman advocate possessed much the same immunity in regard to his utterances as the absolute privilege of a modern barrister in the common-law world—who, however, would simply not be permitted by the court to abuse this privilege in order to injure unfairly a party, a witness or an outsider, and who would be constrained to keep reasonable control over his expressions.

There was in the Roman world no apparent legal notion with a fixed content like the English 'privilege'. (Although Tacitus does expressly refer to the *datum ius*, the 'conceded right', *potentissimum quemque vexandi*,[1] this seems to bear more on the generally unbridled manners of the dying Republic than specifically on modes of court advocacy.) Perhaps J. A. Crook's observation is relevant here: that 'politics and the law courts were accepted by the upper class in Republican times as a game with its own special rules, such that they thought it beneath their dignity to appeal to umpires outside the game about what was said of them by their peers in the course of it'.[2] On the other hand, not all litigants belonged to the upper class, and there would be no reason why they should 'play the game' if they came from a class without such an exquisite sense of dignity, so that something more—as suggested above, an immunity like privilege—is probably needed to explain the coexistence of *vituperatio* and the law of *iniuria*. But even if Crook's attractive idea (reminiscent of Huizinga's view of litigation as a game)[3] were a sufficient explanation of this coexistence, it would still remain true that for the reputable Roman it must have been mortifying to be forced into the role of a player and to have to submit to abuse by his opponent's counsel and to the malicious interest of spectators.

The objection might be raised here that insults uttered in court may have somehow not counted as 'real' insults—not exactly in Crook's sense that they were borne as a matter of pride by the upper class, but in the more general sense that

[1] *Dial.* 40. [2] *Law and Life of Rome* 255.
[3] *Homo Ludens*, ch. 4 ('Der Prozeß als Spiel').

perhaps they were not taken too seriously and so were no real danger to one's *existimatio*. But the sources would in fact entirely invalidate such a suggestion; there is no doubt whatever that court abuse was indeed felt as an attack on *existimatio*. In Cicero's *pro Tullio*, for instance, this appears quite clearly; in this speech Cicero treats his opponent, for once, relatively mildly and without the insults otherwise usual; but he expressly says, when promising at the outset of his speech to abstain from abuse, that this restraint on his part will be for the benefit of his opponent's *fama* and *existimatio*. In Quintilian's manual on rhetoric, which is about 150 years later than Cicero, but which still belongs to what is conventionally called the early classical period of Roman law, we are expressly told[1] that the beginning of a court speech should contain a consideration of the persons involved; and this must involve blackening (*infamandam*) the person on the other side; noticeable here is that Quintilian uses exactly the same word (*infamare*) which denotes, in technical legal usage, something which will ground an *actio iniuriarum*.[2] In two other passages[3] Quintilian uses *infamia* to describe the effect which is achieved by rhetorical abuse of one's opponent or his witnesses. Further passages might be cited to show that this very word *infamia*—injury to one's *fama* or *existimatio*—is applied as the outcome of court *vituperatio*. There can, therefore, be no question of *vituperatio* appearing harmless or not being taken seriously.

Seen from this perspective, the so-called 'praetorian' *infamia* must now assume a slightly different aspect. Clearly it would be wrong to imagine that loss of, or injury to, *existimatio* could arise only in connection with a *iudicium famosum*, an action in which condemnation brought in its train the procedural results called *infamia* in the stricter sense, and that the avoidance of condemnation automatically meant avoiding also any trace of disgrace. On the contrary, anyone who let himself in for litigation, whether as plaintiff or defendant, had to accept a certain loss of face as an inevitable concomitant. The point about 'praetorian' *infamia* seems therefore to be this: that if he was

[1] *Inst. or.* 4. 2. 9. [2] D. 47. 10. 15. 25. [3] *Inst. or.* 7. 2. 28, 5. 7. 26.

condemned in a lawsuit on an issue which the Romans thought of as particularly associated with honour—i.e. in an *actio famosa*—the disgrace, so to speak, was officially, and not merely conventionally, established through the praetor's refusal to admit him thereafter to procedural representation; the loss of face was, so to speak, institutionalized; but this formal 'disgrace' was merely an intensified incidence of the *infamia* or *infamatio* which every litigant risked incurring. It was, in a sense, the participation of the state in marking him as having lost face; but this humiliation differed only in that formal degree from the humiliation which threatened any party to any lawsuit.

Obviously this broad and general conclusion requires modification depending on circumstances. Firstly, it is plain that some kinds of litigation were inherently more potentially painful than others—and here of course the *actiones famosae* are in a quite special category—but there is also a factor, not hitherto much noticed, which must have been also relevant, namely the degree of publicity attending hearings of various kinds. It does not need to be emphasized that hurtful rhetoric or damaging evidence is less fearful the fewer the people are who have access to the proceedings, and it will do no harm to consider whether this observation may contribute something to our understanding of the Roman judicial system.

It has occasionally been asserted that the principle of 'publicity' dominated the conduct of legal proceedings in Rome; Kaser, for example, says that in the earlier period (in contrast to the post-classical period) the publicity of litigation may be taken for granted, but he cites no text in support of this;[1] Bethmann-Hollweg, writing a century earlier, had also said that 'all court proceedings were absolutely public, and access was permitted to every citizen',[2] but equally without supporting texts. Bethmann-Hollweg and Wenger[3] particularize, however, in the case of the *apud iudicem* stage: this (they say) took place in public because the XII Tables said *ni pacunt, in comitio aut in foro ante meridiem causam coiciunto*, and Kaser[4] uses the same

[1] *RZPrR* 9.

[2] *Der römische Civilprozess*, i. 75.

[3] *Institutionen des röm. Zivilprozessrechts*, 72.

[4] *RZPrR* 36.

text, apparently for the same purpose, though with the reservation that perhaps in early times the parties might arrange a place to suit themselves. Kaser adds that, later, the *comitium* alone was used in default of agreement, and relies here on two texts, Cic. *Brut.* 289–90 and Macrob. *Sat.* 3. 16. 15.

So far as the XII Tables passage is concerned, Kaser himself had earlier[1] pointed out that the very next sentence, as reported by Aulus Gellius[2]—*post meridiem praesenti litem addicito*—seems from the characteristic verb *addicere* to refer to the magistrate and not to a *iudex*; and while the usage of the XII Tables is such that the subject of a verb is often left to be understood, and may change even within the same sentence,[3] this particular passage does not amount to a usable piece of evidence about the functioning of a *iudex unus*, quite apart from the difficulty that at the epoch of the XII Tables the *iudex unus* cannot have been the sole kind of judicial organ.[4]

The Cicero passage[5] is a curious and difficult one. It occurs at a point where Cicero describes the miserably thin style of certain orators who consider themselves 'Attic'. He goes on:

> Qua re si anguste et exiliter dicere est Atticorum, sint sane Attici; sed in comitium veniant, ad stantem iudicem dicant; subsellia grandiorem et pleniorem vocem desiderant. Volo hoc oratori contingat, ut cum auditum sit eum esse dicturum, locus in subselliis occupetur, compleatur tribunal, gratiosi scribae sint in dando et cedendo loco, corona multiplex, iudex erectus; cum surgat is qui dicturus sit, significetur a corona silentium, deinde crebrae assensiones, multae admirationes; risus cum velit, cum velit fletus . . .

So far as concerns the bearing of this passage on the question whether proceedings *apud iudicem* were necessarily or generally

[1] *Festschrift Wenger*, i. 117 ff. [2] *N.A.* 17. 2. 10.

[3] e.g. the opening sentences in Table I as conventionally reconstructed.

[4] There is also the question—raised by the use of this XII Tables passage—whether at the period of the XII Tables the familiar bipartition of civil lawsuits between magistrate and *iudex* had already taken place and been generalized. The evidence of the XII Tables itself—basically no more than the *legis actio per iudicis postulationem* attributed to it by Gaius, *Inst.* 4. 17a—certainly is to the effect that bipartition was known at least in certain cases, but seems, from the fact that only certain cases are mentioned, not necessarily to have been generalized. Conceivably, then, in other cases the entire case was heard and decided by the magistrate.

[5] *Brutus* 289–90.

public, the latter part, from 'volo' onwards, is evidently irrelevant. It is true that there is the word 'iudex' in the singular; but weighed against this are, firstly, the word *tribunal*, characteristic only of a magistrate[1] and particularly of a praetor,[2] and secondly, the reference to *scribae*, attendants again characteristic of a magistrate and not of a *iudex*. These indications, it seems to me, compel the conclusion either that *iudex erectus* must be a mere turn of speech conveying in fact a body of judges, as one might speak in English, even in describing a plurality of listeners, of the reactions of 'the hearer' rather than of 'the audience', or that *iudex* is in fact the *iudex quaestionis* or presiding magistrate at a *quaestio*-trial. The first part of the passage is not so easy to dispose of; we find a *iudex* apparently operating in the public *comitium*. But what kind of *iudex* is he? It may be that, with the reference to *comitium*, Cicero intended the word to mean 'magistrate', since apparently early usage permitted the word *iudex* to include a magistrate[3] and, as has just been said, even later usage permitted it to bear this sense in the title *iudex quaestionis*.[4] The word *stantem* does not fit a magistrate very well, as he would normally be seated on his *sella curulis*; unless indeed what is meant by *stantem* is something like *de plano*, i.e. what is aimed at by Cicero is to make graphic a very simple piece of pleading in a trivial and uncontentious matter such as the praetor might dispose of if one halted him on his way to or from the *tribunal*. *Ad stantem iudicem dicant* may then just possibly be intended to describe pleading before a magistrate and, if so, of course it would be irrelevant to the question of the publicity of proceedings *apud iudicem* in the strict sense. But if *iudicem* really does mean a private person, not a magistrate, *stantem* is even harder to explain. Kunkel[5] uses the passage to ground the assumption that cases which did not need a long hearing were dealt with by a *iudex* who decided them, literally, on his feet; this is also the view of Gioffredi.[6]

[1] Weiss, *RE* s.v. *tribunal*.

[2] Gioffredi, 9 *SDHI* (1943) 230 ff.

[3] Livy 3. 55; Cicero *De leg*. 3. 8.

[4] Kunkel, *Kriminalverfahren*, 48; Jones, *The Criminal Courts of the Roman Republic and Principate*, 55, 128 nn. 86, 87.

[5] 85 *ZSS* 320 n.

[6] Op. cit. 242.

If they are right, the 'court' of the *iudex stans* must certainly have been of absolutely minimal significance—and of course this would suit the argument in Cicero's mind, viz. that poor orators should confine themselves to arguing short and trivial cases—and would certainly not be resorted to by anyone with some serious litigation on his hands requiring witnesses, documents, and so forth. Accordingly, whichever way we look at this passage, it is of no value in advancing the idea that proceedings *apud iudicem* were basically public.

The other passage used by Kaser is Macrobius *Sat.* 3. 16. 15, in which we have a purported quotation from a Republican orator, C. Titius, speaking on the *lex Fannia* (a sumptuary law of 161 B.C.) and describing how several convivial men make their drunken way, after various excesses, to the forum to act as *iudices*:

> Inde ad comitium vadunt, ne litem suam faciant. Dum eunt, nulla est in angiporto amphora quam non impleant, quippe qui vesicam plenam vini habeant. Veniunt in comitium, tristes iubent dicere. Quorum negotium est, narrant, iudex testes poscit, ipsus it minctum. Ubi redit, ait se omnia audivisse, tabulas poscit, litteras inspicit: vix prae vino sustinet palpebras. Eunt in consilium. Ibi haec oratio: 'quid mihi negotii est cum istis nugatoribus, quin potius potamus mulsum mixtum vino Graeco, edimus turdam pinguem bonumque piscem, lupum germanum qui inter duos pontes captus fuit?'

This passage certainly describes a court hearing in the *comitium*, but it is equally certainly not the *apud iudicem* stage of a *iudicium privatum*, as the judges mentioned are evidently sitting as, or as part of, a collegiate court—either the *centumviri* or a *quaestio*, more likely the former.[1] Apart from their general behaviour beforehand, suggesting that they all had the same programme for the day, there is the judge who goes away to answer a call of nature immediately after having called for the testimony of witnesses; this must imply (since on his return the evidence has been given) that other judges were still hearing the case during his absence; anything else would be absurd even beyond the

[1] The references to *tabulae* and to the parties as *nugatores* (triflers) as well as to *litem suam facere* suggest a civil rather than a criminal issue; and if both criminal justice and the *unus iudex* are excluded, I would understand *tabulae* as meaning the *tabulae* of a will.

absurdity at which the orator is pitching his description. Then, *eunt in consilium*; this must mean that they withdraw to consider their verdict. One might of course insist that *eunt in consilium* means that each judge (each being a *iudex unus* trying a separate case) retired with his own *consilium*, but the passage mentions no separate *consilia*; moreover, how likely is it that a series of *iudicia privata* would reach judgment stage at precisely the same time? Finally, the talk in the *consilium* about eating and drinking fits far more naturally into the supposition that the *consilium* in fact consists of the very people who had been enjoying one another's company a short while ago, before public duty called them away.

Apart from these passages used by Kaser, there are some others (cited by Bethmann-Hollweg)[1] which might be thought to bear on the matter; thus e.g. Suetonius *Aug.* 29:

> Publica opera plurima exstruxit, e quibus vel praecipua: forum cum aede Martis Ultoris, templum Apollinis in Palatio, aedem Tonantis Jovis in Capitolio. Fori exstruendi causa fuit hominum et iudiciorum multitudo, quae videbatur non sufficientibus duobus etiam tertio indigere: itaque festinatius necdum perfecta Martis aede publicatum est cautumque, ut separatim in eo publica iudicia et sortitiones iudicum fierent.

One reading of this passage might hint that, as the new forum was devoted to *iudicia publica* and *sortitiones iudicum*, no other activity was to take place there except these, which would then be conducted separately from (presumably) other legal proceedings, i.e. *iudicia privata* in the other *fora*. But such an interpretation of the passage seems unlikely. We are, after all, told that the new forum was needed because of overcrowding not just through lawsuits but also simply through *multitudo hominum*, and presumably therefore the new forum would allow for an overflow of ordinary traffic as well as of lawsuits (it contained, after all, a temple). The passage would be better understood if it were taken to mean that, in the new forum, a certain area, aside from the ordinary hubbub of traffic, was reserved for *iudicia publica* and *sortitiones*; this would be the force of *separatim*, and no implied distinction between these and *iudicia privata* in

[1] Op. cit. ii. 162–3.

the other *fora* need be seen. And indeed, if one goes this distance in interpreting the passage in this direction, it would even amount to a mild hint that *iudicia privata* were of no significance so far as concerned the adequacy or otherwise of the city's open spaces.

These three *fora* are mentioned by Seneca in an inflated passage of censure on the times:[1]

Numquam irasci desinet sapiens, si semel coeperit . . . [There follows a picture of the contemporary evils of society, ending:] Adde nunc publica periuria gentium et rupta foedera et in praedam validioris quidquid non resistebat abductum, circumscriptiones, furta, fraudes, infitiationes, quibus trina non sufficiunt fora.

In fact the four matters *quibus trina non sufficiunt fora* could all be identified with elements in civil law: *circumscriptio* is used of the cheating of a minor[2] or overreaching someone by defeating the purpose of a will;[3] *furta* are civil delicts; *fraudes* might conceivably allude to *alienationes in fraudem creditorum*, or to *fraus patroni*; and *infitiationes* might be a hint of the *infitiatio* which caused a doubling of the *lis* in certain cases.[4] On the other hand, they are equally all expressions which might refer to activity coming to light in a criminal setting. One of them at least—*furta*—is highly unlikely to mean literally cases ending in the civil *actio furti*, which by Seneca's time was virtually a dead letter;[5] moreover, *infitiatio* is twice used by Cicero to mean denying a criminal charge,[6] and *fraudes* and *circumscriptiones* may easily be understood as extortion, peculation, or forgery. But the strongest argument against assuming an allusion here to *iudicia privata* lies in a rhetorical consideration; the exaggerated picture of evil conditions drawn by Seneca in the entire passage would be weakened ridiculously if the climactic words are taken to mean situations typically non-criminal but civil—if, instead of a heightening of colour as the passage ends, we get a feeble declension from *publica periuria gentium et rupta foedera* to something which can be understood as meaning a mere disputing of

[1] *De ira* 2. 9. 1–4.
[2] e.g. Julian, D. 21. 2. 39. pr.
[3] Pliny *Ep.* 8. 18. 4.
[4] Kaser, *RZPrR* 99, 298.
[5] Kelly, *Roman Litigation*, 161 ff.
[6] *De orat.* 2. 25. 105; *Orat. part.* 29. 102.

liability in an action for negligence under the *lex Aquilia*.[1] The passage must therefore be judged of no weight as an argument for the general publicity of civil litigation.

As against these passages adduced by Bethmann-Hollweg and Kaser—to such poor effect, as has been seen—there are four other texts of which three offer no more than slight hints that *iudicia privata* could and did take place otherwise than in public, while the fourth is quite unambiguous in this direction.

The first two both describe the participation of Tiberius in the administration of justice despite his evident determination not to interfere with it directly.[2] In the case of *quaestio*-trials Suetonius says:[3] *Si quem reorum elabi gratia rumor esset, subitus aderat iudicesque aut e plano aut e quaesitoris tribunali et religionis et noxae, de qua cognoscerent, admonebat*. In the case of the praetor's judicial activity (perhaps while presiding over a *quaestio*) Tacitus tells us[4] that: *nec patrum cognitionibus satiatus iudiciis adsidebat in cornu tribunalis, ne praetorem curuli depelleret; multaque eo coram adversus ambitum et potentium preces constituta*. Perhaps it is worth observing, even as an *argumentum ex silentio*, that both authors show us Tiberius as intervening only in cases of a criminal kind, or possibly also in cases which were still at the *in iure* stage before the praetor; i.e. in cases which are known certainly to have been accessible to the public. There is no reference to his using his influence to counteract *ambitus* or *gratia* at the *apud iudicem* stage of *iudicia privata*, where these elements might also be at work:[5] an indication, even if a slight one, that these *iudicia* were usually or very often tried privately?

There is also Cicero, *pro Quinctio* 53, a passage in which he says to his client's adversary that if he had been less merciless, less unbecomingly quick to stand on his uttermost rights, he would not now have been reduced *in eam turpitudinem . . . ut hoc tibi esset apud tales viros confitendum, qua tibi vadimonium non sit obitum, eadem te hora consilium cepisse hominis propinqui fortunas funditus evertere*. This case was tried by a *iudex unus* (C. Aquilius Gallus),

[1] D. 9. 2. 2. 1, 9. 2. 23. 10; Gaius *Inst*. 3. 216.
[2] Kelly, *Princeps Iudex*, 23, 47.
[3] *Tiberius* 33.
[4] *Ann*. 1. 75.
[5] Kelly, *Roman Litigation*, 31 ff.

who was surrounded by his *consilium* of three: L. Lucilius, P. Quinctilius, and M. Marcellus. The disgrace in which Cicero depicts Naevius as involved consists in having to admit his malevolence before four such distinguished men (*apud tales viros*); but surely one might imagine, had there been a *corona* of bystanders listening to the action, that Cicero's rhetorical instinct would have suggested to him to say that the disgrace was deepened by its disclosure to the public at large as well? This (admittedly) very tenuous reflection would suggest that the action between Quinctius and Naevius was heard, in fact, in private.

Finally there is the clear testimony of Vitruvius, the famous architect of the first century B.C. He describes[1] how the houses of noblemen should be built: there must be a certain degree of splendour about them, *quod in domibus eorum saepius et publica consilia et privata iudicia arbitriaque conficiuntur*. This is the clearest possible proof that *iudicia privata* could and did take place, literally, in private; within the four walls of a private house.[2]

This conclusion has been reached also by Kunkel and Behrends in recently published works[3] on the basis of the Vitruvius passage, but it seemed worth while to reinforce it by looking critically, as has been done above, at the passages adduced by other writers in support of the general 'publicity' idea.[4] It would be unreasonable to assert that all *iudicia privata* necessarily took place in private, but evidently some, perhaps most, did.[5]

1 *De arch.* 6. 5. 2.

2 Aulus Gellius (*N.A.* 14. 2) describes a lawsuit over an alleged money debt which he had to hear when appointed to judge *iudicia privata*. He adjourned the case in perplexity to go and take the advice of a philosopher, and he puts this as follows: *A subselliis pergo ire ad Favorinum philosophum*. The reference to *subsellia* would certainly suggest, at first sight, a hearing in one of the public halls on the Forum, but in view of the Vitruvius passage one could equally imagine that *subsellia* would be found also in a nobleman's private house, which was to contain (says Vitruvius in the same passage) *basilicas non dissimili modo quam publicorum operum magnificentia ⟨habeant⟩ comparatas*. These rooms would therefore be pretty big; and Vitruvius says they would be expected to accommodate *publica consilia*.

3 Kunkel, 85 *ZSS* 320 n.; Behrends, *Geschworenenverfassung*, 93 n.

4 Other passages used for this purpose are Seneca, *Contr.* 9 *praef.* 3, and *De ira* 3. 33. 1–2.

5 In the later Empire there are explicit admonitions from Constantine (C. Th. 1. 12. 1) and Valentinian and Valens (C. Th. 1. 16. 9) that all cases are to

Apart from the passages which have just been examined, a further indication that varying degrees of publicity attended the hearing of *iudicia privata* lies in the advice contained in Roman writings on rhetoric, to the effect that one's style ought to be adapted to one's audience. One good example is provided by Cicero:[1] *Quam enim indecorum est, de stillicidiis cum apud unum iudicem dicas, amplissimis verbis et locis uti communibus, de maiestate populi Romani summisse et subtiliter!* Grand words, impressive clichés are not appropriate when pleading about a trivial easement before a single judge, any more than plain and modest language would be suitable to a treason trial. It may be suspected that the point is simply—as any university lecturer knows—that one should adapt one's tone to the size of one's audience rather than to the importance of the subject-matter,[2] and that to use a style of harangue with a class of three or four would be ridiculous, or *indecorum*, while it may easily be the only way to engage a class of a hundred or so. Cicero's correspondence contains another hint to the same effect:[3] *quin ipsa iudicia non solemus omnia tractare uno modo. Privatas causas et eas tenuis agimus subtilius, capitis aut famae scilicet ornatius.* And the same commonplace of rhetorical wisdom is mentioned by Quintilian.[4] A final passage from Cicero, in which rhetorical style is expressly related to the size of the audience, seems to put this matter beyond doubt:[5] *Sed si eodem modo putant exercitu in foro et in omnibus templis, quae circum forum sunt, conlocato dici pro Milone decuisse, ut si de re privata ad unum iudicem diceremus, vim eloquentiae sua facultate, non rei natura metiuntur.* With an 'army' of spectators packing the forum and the surrounding buildings, it would have been unfitting to use the same style in defending Milo on a charge of criminal violence as if one were pleading a private issue before a single judge.

be heard in public and not *in secessu domus*; this suggests an attempt to impose a 'publicity principle' on a practice which leaned more towards privacy.

[1] *Orator* 72.

[2] It is true that Cicero does expressly mention adapting one's style to *id quod agemus* (*De orat.* 3. 212), but the *id* can be interpreted as meaning the whole circumstances of the hearing. The legal issue involved would technically be *res de qua agitur*.

[3] *Ad fam.* 9. 21. 1.

[4] *Inst. orat.* 4. 1. 57; 5. 10. 115.

[5] *De opt. gen. orat.* 4. 10.

# V

# The *Unus Iudex*

THE technique I have adopted, in trying to present an organized picture of the Roman Republican judicature, has been the reverse of the usual: instead of starting with the *unus iudex* (thus giving him a position of apparent primacy which may in many respects be deserved but which tends to throw the whole picture out of focus by casting the *centumviri* and *recuperatores* as subsidiary phenomena), I have left him to the end. Starting with the *centumviri* I have tried to account for the separate existence and jurisdiction of this court which contrasts, in composition and procedure, so strongly with the *unus iudex*; then I have tried to discover the nature of *recuperatores* by pointing to a factor which might explain their curious and very specialized functions. In doing this, it will be seen that I have, by negative implication, foreshadowed certain characteristics of the *unus iudex* inasmuch as the factors which form the *ratio* of the *centumviri* or *recuperatores* will not be present in his case. I then tried, in two further chapters, to fill out our background knowledge of Roman litigation generally, so as to suggest, firstly, the relative quantitative importance which the *unus iudex* (and the other courts) may have had in the dispatch of judicial business, and secondly the likelihood that the Roman shyness about litigation may provide some understanding of the nature of the *iudicium privatum*, the lawsuit determined by the *unus iudex*. It is now time, after these various oblique approaches, to meet the *unus iudex* and the *iudicium privatum* head on.

An analysis of the expression *iudicium privatum* must begin from the observation that the opposition *privatus/publicus* was an extremely commonplace thought in the Roman world, evidently to the same extent and with something like the same spectrum of meaning as the contrast private/public in modern English.

There are several contexts in which the opposition is frequent: firstly, the context of public as opposed to private law, or public as opposed to private rights;[1] secondly, the context in which *privatus* is meant to denote the capacity of a private citizen as distinct from an official capacity;[2] thirdly, the context in which something like 'private arrangements' is intended;[3] fourthly, a context like that of the English word 'private' in the sense of 'secluded', 'not done or held in public';[4] and finally the strict procedural context in which *privatus, -a, -um* is used to qualify nouns implying litigation in some form.[5]

The view is held by some philologists and legal historians that *privatus* must be understood as a participle of *privo, -are* and that the central sense requires the word *imperio* to be understood, i.e. one who is *privatus* is 'deprived' of magistral powers—*imperio privatus*. Thus, for example, Walde–Hofmann[6] give *privatus* as meaning *privatus imperio* and cite in support 'the fuller formula *sine imperio privatus*' from the *lex Ursonensis*,[7] and this interpretation recurs among the legal historians. But in fact it seems very unlikely. For instance, the *senatusconsultum de Bacanalibus* (186 B.C., nearly a century and a half earlier than the *lex Ursonensis* of 44 B.C.) uses the word not merely absolutely, but adverbially and in a context where the addition of anything like the notion of *imperium* would not improve the meaning: *neve in poplicod neve in preivatod neve exstrad urbem sacra quisque fecise velet.* Moreover, the vast preponderance of the *privatus-* passages in all of Latin literature are ones in which it seems easier to understand the word as having a basic meaning very much

[1] e.g. Plaut. *Capt.* 334–5, *Curc.* 552, *Trin.* 38, 287; Varro *R.R.* 3. 2. 1; Cic. *De inv.* 1. 11–12, 1. 35; *Har. resp.* 14, 16; *Rhet. Her.* 4. 36. 48; Hor. *Ars poetica* 131; Livy 2. 55. 8, 25. 18. 5, 9; Gellius 11. 18. 18.

[2] e.g. Cato *Or. frg.* (Ford) 56; Varro *L.L.* 6. 86, 91, 92; 9. 68; Cic. *De inv.* 2. 92; Gellius 13. 12. 6, 7.

[3] e.g. Varro *L.L.* 5. 4. 2; Cic. *De sen.* 21; Gellius 7. 6. 10 (if indeed this is a category validly distinguishable from the foregoing).

[4] e.g. Livy 2. 54. 7, 34. 2. 10, 39. 18. 6; Cic. *De inv.* 1. 38; Suet. *Div. Iul.* 18.

[5] e.g. Cic. *Rhet. Her.* 1. 12. 22; *Q. Rosc.* 16; *Verr.* 2. 2. 75; *Cluent.* 163; *Flacc.* 12; *De domo* 108; *Div. Caec.* 18; *Brutus* 178, 217, 238, 246, 311; *Orator* 129; Val. Max. 8. 2. 2; Gellius 14. 2. 1–8; and numerous other passages.

[6] *Lateinisches etymologisches Wörterbuch*, 3rd edn., 363.

[7] Cols. 130, 131.

the same as the modern English 'private'—pertaining to an individual and his affairs as such—and so to be some extension of *privus* rather than a participle of *privare* requiring the silent addition of *imperio* in order to be understood. Even the passage from the *lex Ursonensis* cited by Walde–Hofmann seems almost to disprove their theory: what they call a 'vollere Formel', *sine imperio privatus*, is—so it seems to me—not a fuller formula for *imperio privatus* at all, but a meticulous expression, characteristic of the prolixity of late Republican legislation, in which the person envisaged is beyond all doubt to be a private individual (*privatus*) and one without magistral powers (*sine imperio*).

In the procedural setting, the incorrectness of the interpretation *privatus* = *privatus imperio* is strikingly illuminated by the fact that the phrase *iudex privatus* occurs very much less frequently than does *iudicium privatum*. In the whole of Roman secular literature *iudex privatus* is found in only four passages,[1] all of them, in the literary sense, post-classical; while *iudicium privatum* occurs in twenty-two passages, twelve of them from Cicero,[2] and equivalent expressions such as *causa privata, lis privata, rei privatae* (*iudex*) are very common.[3] If the sense of *privatus* were really felt as participial, from *privare*, surely this disproportion would be reversed; *iudex privatus* (sc. *imperio*) would be the original and earlier expression, and the abstractions *iudicium privatum*, etc., would be the secondary and later derivations (since *iudicium imperio privatum* does not seem to make good primary sense). Kaser correctly observed[4] the rarity of the expression *iudex privatus*, but does not comment on its infrequency when specifically compared with *iudicium privatum*, saying merely that *iudex privatus* means the 'single' judge,

[1] Tac. *Ann.* 14. 28. 4; Suet. *Claud.* 14; Quint. *Inst.* 5. 10. 114–15; Gellius, *N.A.* 14. 2. 8.

[2] Cic. *De inv.* 2. 58; *Cluent.* 74, 163; *Q. Rosc.* 16; *Verr.* 2. 2. 75; *Flacc.* 12; *De dom.* 108; *Post red. in sen.* 21; *De orat.* 173–4, 178–9; *Brutus* 217; *Top.* 17. 65; Nepos *Them.* 1. 3; Vitruv. 6. 8 (5). 2. 3; Sen. *contr.* 7. 1 (16). 22; 7. 2 (17). 7–8; *De clem.* 1. 9–10; Quint. *Inst.* 4. 2. 61–2, 6. 4. 7, 11. 3. 150; Pliny *Ep.* 6. 33. 7–9; Gell. *N.A.* 14. 2. 1.

[3] e.g.: Cic. *De inv.* 1. 3–4; *Q. Rosc.* 24–5; *Verr.* 2. 2. 71; *De orat.* 1. 202, 2. 100; *Brut.* 177, 238, 245–6, 311–12, 322; *De opt. gen. or.* 4. 10–11; *Ep. ad fam.* 9. 21. 1; Ovid *Tristia* 2. 95; Val. Max. 7. 8. 7; Quint. *Decl.* 266.

[4] *RZPrR* 34 n. 23.

*iudicium privatum* the case tried by the single judge. It is perfectly true that the *iudicium privatum* was essentially associated with the single judge;[1] but when the intention was to emphasize that the judicial organ was one man and not a plurality, the expression apparently more naturally used was *unus iudex*. Thus, for instance, Cicero in a passage already mentioned in another connection contrasts the style of rhetoric appropriate to a great state trial (that of Milo for the murder of Clodius) with the style appropriate *si de re privata ad unum iudicem diceremus*;[2] and in a similar contrast in rhetorical styles he instances hypothetically the case where *de stillicidiis cum apud unum iudicem dicas*.[3] Accordingly the conclusion must be that *privatus* in a procedural setting not only has nothing to do with the notion of *privatus imperio* (a phrase found, as an independent concept, nowhere in Roman literature)—as Kaser evidently accepts—but also is not primarily a reflection of the numerical singularity of the judicial organ. What is central to the *iudicium privatum* is not the fact that it is tried by a single judge—this, though true, is secondary—but that it is 'private' in a certain sense, which it now remains to explore.

If this interpretation is kept for the moment in mind, a curious result ensues. It is that, although one might have thought that family affairs, such as those connected with an inheritance, would be reckoned as *res privatae*, and a lawsuit arising from them as a *lis privata* or *iudicium privatum*, in fact this is not the case. Evidently a distinction existed—more subtle, at first sight, than the English distinction between 'private' and 'public'—between certain classes of dispute, all of which would, for us, belong to the sphere of 'private' law. For instance, we have a very clear testimony from Pliny[4] that trials held in the centumviral court were not classified as *iudicia privata*; and, since the idea that *privatus* means 'single' has been rejected, evidently the criterion on which centumviral trials were distinguished from *iudicia privata* was something more than

[1] Ibid. Cases tried by *centumviri* or *recuperatores*, although of 'private law' content in the Roman or in the modern sense, are never called *iudicia privata*.

[2] *De opt. gen. orat.* 4. 10.

[3] *Orator* 72.

[4] *Ep.* 6. 33. 9.

the fact merely that they were conducted before a plurality of judges: in describing what is clearly an unusual centumviral case,[1] he says that, while it was going on, recourse had to be had to numerical calculations, to such a degree *ut repente in privati iudicii formam centumvirale vertatur*. The same distinction appears in the passage from Cicero already discussed above, in which the impertinent novice orator is described as (a) haunting the magistrates' tribunals; (b) *iudicia privata magnarum rerum obire*; and (c) *iactare se in causis centumviralibus*.[2]

A similar observation can be made in contrasting the *iudicium privatum*, with its characteristic *unus iudex*, with the *iudicium recuperatorium*: the latter is never described in the sources as being *privatum*. Again there is a criterion hidden in the usage (though not too deeply hidden in this instance) by which the idea central to the *iudicium privatum* is absent from the *iudicium recuperatorium*; and, just as with the contrast with the *centumviri* mentioned above, this distinction does not rest on the numerical plurality of the *recuperatores*.

Certainly, there are very obvious elements in the centumviral and recuperatorial jurisdictions which—although the material within their competences would today be labelled 'private' law—might well explain superficially why centumviral and recuperatorial trials were not classified as *iudicia privata*. In the former case, where inheritance problems were in issue, it might be enough to cite the dictum of Papinian,[3] *testamenti factio non privati, sed publici iuris est*; and indeed the whole theory of the centumviral jurisdiction which I have tried to establish rests on the conception of a public interest being involved in the descent of a *hereditas*. In the latter case, the exceptional nature of the procedure is explained also by the element of public interest, even if an interest of a quite different kind. But note that the contrast to which I am drawing attention does not result from any conscious Roman classification of centumviral and recuperatorial proceedings on those grounds (they are

[1] Unusual, because all four panels of judges, totalling 180, heard the case: ibid. 3.

[2] *De orat.* I. 173.

[3] D. 28. I. 3.

nowhere called *iudicia publica* or anything like that; this phrase carried an entirely different meaning), but from the evidently well-understood conception of the *iudicium privatum*. This conception arises, not by conscious opposition to centumviral or recuperatorial trials, or even to *iudicia publica*, but as a depiction of a judicial arrangement with its own special reasons for existing.

If we are to approach an understanding of this conception, it must be done, I think, via a number of observations for some of which the ground has already been laid. But the first observation is one not so far made or suggested: the extraordinary multiplicity, or fluidity, in the nomenclature of the *iudicia privata* and of the personages who conducted them. Efforts have been made to sort the various types of private *iudicium* and judge into categories with a material basis, and, while these efforts do not all agree, there is no doubt that a variety of materially different conceptions underlies the variety in names. At the same time I call attention to this very variety as being significant; it does not, after all, exist in the fields which we have identified as being 'centumviral' or 'recuperatorial'. It suggests to me that the 'private' element in the system centred on the single judge included a 'privacy' of choice which existed outside the spheres in which one kind of public interest or another demanded the intervention of *centumviri* or *recuperatores*. The single judge was a polymorphous phenomenon, and the form in which he played his part was something in which the state evidently took little or no interest, preferring to leave it to the disposition of the parties to determine.

It seems to be settled doctrine[1] that the notions of *iudex* and *arbiter*, originally separate in that the *iudex* decided contested issues of fact or fault, as against the more limited function of the *arbiter* in assessing the amount of money due on an issue not otherwise contested, or in acting as umpire in issues (such as the division of an inheritance) in which the parties are not in postures of mutual opposition, were fused in that the *iudex* took over the functions originally peculiar to the *arbiter*. When *arbiter*

[1] See Kaser *RZPrR* 41.

turns up as a separate phenomenon later, what is meant, according to the current doctrine, is that certain relationships, notably the *bonae fidei* relationships and the actions with a *clausula arbitraria*, were submitted to a 'private' *arbiter* or umpire, and that this proceeding was gradually taken under official control. It may, however, be observed that if the history of these two conceptions was really as represented—i.e. as a process with results clearly defined by the time of the rise of the formulary procedure—it would be hard to account for the extreme looseness of language among people who, even if not jurists, must still have known enough law to grasp such simple distinctions. If we look at Cicero's witticisms at the expense of the legal profession in his speech *pro Murena*[1] we find that after an extended and sarcastic description of the follies of the civil lawyers he says 'and yet after such long experience these clever men are not able to make up their minds whether one ought to say *dies tertius* or *perendinus*, *iudex* or *arbiter*, *res* or *lis*'. Now it is true, as Broggini points out,[2] that Cicero did not expect this passage to be taken seriously; he had been (he wrote later in *De finibus* 74) 'playing to the gallery', but even a joke loses its savour unless a certain verisimilitude is kept up, and it seems to me that Broggini is wrong to represent, no doubt inadvertently, this closing part of the passage as being the words particularly referred to in the *De finibus* rather than the passage as a whole—in which setting there is no reason to take every legal allusion as being facetious and so misleading. It was, of course, Broggini's purpose to show the essential technical distinction, still present at the end of the Republic, between *iudex* and *arbiter*, so that he was bound to minimize anything which might suggest their identity, such as *pro Murena* 27, where the terms are treated as virtually interchangeable, or as much so as the pairs *perendinus dies*/*tertius dies* or *lis*/*res*. The point to which, on the other hand, I want to call attention is not the probative value of *pro Murena* 27 for the proposition that *iudex* and *arbiter* were *really* indistinguishable, but its probative value for the much humbler proposition that in ordinary speech—the everyday tongue of

[1] 27. [2] *Iudex Arbiterve*, 199 f.

the *corona*—both terms reflected a rather undifferentiated concept. Note, for instance, that Cicero did not think of suggesting that the pair of ideas *iudex/recuperator* could not be easily distinguished, although this pair of words, or their corresponding abstracts, used in juxtaposition would not have been totally strange to his audience; they occurred in the *lex agraria* as well as in provincial legislation which may possibly have had some metropolitan model,[1] and turn up several times in Cicero's own speeches.[2]

*Arbiter* in the strict sense is found, as has been said, in contexts like the *bonae fidei iudicia*, or the *clausula arbitraria*; but this judicial personage is divided, by a frontier which is shadowy enough, from a 'purely' private *arbiter*, arranged between the parties to a dispute without reference to the magistrate, and on the basis of an exchange of stipulations as to the observance of the *arbiter*'s award (*ex compromisso*).[3] This, at any rate, is the general doctrine. Yet the expression *arbiter ex compromisso* is extremely rare;[4] and when this rarity is compared with the relative frequency of *arbiter* or *arbitrium* (without qualification), it is evident that the technical distinction between an *arbiter* whose finding was the result of a magistral directive, and an *arbiter* whose finding would come under magistral notice only if it were disobeyed and the disobedient party's stipulation were sued on, did not seem important. It was a distinction which the circumstances of the parties might find serviceable, but which was altogether subordinate to the essential privacy of choice, where such details were concerned, in any matter falling generally outside the public-interest-oriented jurisdictions of *centumviri* and *recuperatores*.

This lack of public interest (merely the obverse of the essentially private interest) as a feature of the single judge's operation

[1] *L. agraria* 34, 35; *l. Antonia de Termessibus* II has *iudicia recuperationes*. The *Fragmentum Atestinum* has *iudicia arbitri recuperatorum datio*.

[2] *Pro Caecina* 8: *iudex recuperatorve*; *Verr.* 2. 3. 135: *coepit* Scandilius *recuperatores aut iudicem postulare*; ibid. 138: *iudicem aut recuperatorem nullum posse reperiri*; *Pro Caecina* 61: *non reperies iudicem aut recuperatorem*.

[3] See Behrends, *Geschworenenverfassung* 122 ff.

[4] It, or a phrase containing its essence, is found only seven times in the Digest: see *VIR* s.v. *compromissum*.

seems to me to be signalized by an expression intended by Cicero to cover all forms of this function: *disceptator domesticus*. It is an expression which Behrends,[1] for instance, would apply only to private, unofficial arbitrators; indeed, he thinks Costa's[2] judgment 'strange' because Costa believed the expression included the *unus iudex* in the strict sense. But if one looks at the whole passage concerned (*pro Caecina* 6), and not merely the first part of it, it is clear that the phrase has a wider significance:

> . . . Omnia iudicia aut distrahendarum controversiarum, aut puniendorum maleficiorum caussa reperta sunt; quorum alterum levius est, propterea quod et minus laedit, et persaepe disceptatore domestico diiudicatur; alterum est vehementissimum, quod et ad graviores res pertinet, et non honorariam operam amici, sed severitatem iudicis ac vim requirit. . . . Nunc vero quis est qui aut vim hominibus armatis factam relinqui putet oportere, aut eius rei leniorem actionem nobis aliquam demonstrare possit?

Now if one looks only at the first part of the passage—that cited by Behrends—it seems as though a simple distinction is being drawn between what I may call a friendly arbitration informally carried through by an agreed umpire, on the one hand, and, on the other hand, a contest 'at arm's length' in which the *iudex* is supposed to be tough. (Even this is scarcely a convincing exegesis of these isolated lines, because they do after all purport to classify *omnia iudicia*, and it is hard to fit, let us say, a strongly contested issue on sale or hire either into the 'friendly settlement' category or into the category of *maleficia* calling for punishment; in other words, the *domestice disceptata* (as so understood) and the *maleficia punienda* seem to leave a lot of important middle ground unaccounted for.) But in fact this part of the speech is used only to introduce the point at which Cicero is aiming: namely the contrast between the kind of jurisdiction which his client is being blamed for invoking (that of *recuperatores*, to whom the expressions *maleficia* and *severitatem iudicis ac vim* are quite appropriate when the cause of action is, as here, *vis hominibus armatis facta*), and the kind of jurisdiction to which his adversary says he ought to have had recourse (the *lenior actio*, the *facilius*

[1] Op. cit. 123, and n. 28.

[2] *Profilo storico del processo civile Romano*, 67.

*et commodius iudicium*,[1] which must mean one conducted by a single judge). Viewed in this way, it seems to me that *disceptator domesticus* is simply a compendious expression meaning one who —disregarding the technical variants in his function[2]—settles the issue in what may be the decent, respectable privacy of his own house.[3] I say 'may be', because the text qualifies the operation of the *disceptator domesticus* with *persaepe*; the implied, unusual occasions on which an issue ranking as a *controversia distrahenda* (rather than a *maleficium puniendum*) would not be handled in this way would be perhaps occasions of the centumviral jurisdiction or of an *unus iudex* sitting, exceptionally, in public.

With this observation we find ourselves alongside the theme of the chapter on the general distaste for litigation which, as we saw, is associated with the 'loss of face' necessarily involved in having one's affairs thrashed out in public and having to submit to the offensive rhetoric of one's adversary's counsel. Instantly a most significant dimension of the *iudicium privatum*, and simultaneously a secondary explanation of its name, leap into the field of strong probability: single-judge litigation could be conducted away from the public view; in private, or, to use a modern expression conveying the nearest judicial equivalent, 'in camera'.

A second element which some texts appear to associate with the *unus iudex* as something, not indeed essential to his definition, but so conspicuous in his functioning as to have a probable significance for the nature of his jurisdiction, is that of business (in the commercial or strictly pecuniary sense). It is true that the earliest evidence of the operation of the single judge shows him as adjudicating, *inter alia*, in the division of an estate[4]—something which in the era of the XII Tables would not have had a particularly 'commercial' flavour—but the Gaius passage in question mentions primarily, as the field of the judge in the *legis actio per iudicis postulationem*, actions based on a stipulation,

[1] *Pro Caecina* 8.

[2] Whether as *iudex* or *arbiter* of whichever kind.

[3] See above, pp. 110 ff.

[4] Gaius *Inst.* 4. 17a: *item de hereditate dividenda inter coheredes eadem lex* [*XII tabularum*] *per iudicis postulationem agi iussit.*

and chooses to give, as an example of the whole *legis actio*, the words used in framing a claim based on a formal promise (*sponsio*) to pay 10,000 sesterces.

In Cicero's speech *pro Cluentio* there is a well-known passage, to which I shall soon return in a different context, in which, as it seems to me, the close or typical association of *unus iudex* and *pecuniariae causae* is suggested: *Neminem voluerunt maiores nostri non modo de existimatione cuiusquam, sed ne pecuniaria quidem de re minima esse iudicem, nisi qui inter adversarios convenisset.*[1] Taken alone, this sentence might suggest a large spectrum of jurisdiction entrusted to the single judge, and of course it is known that in some cases which were heard by him the *existimatio* of the defendant was especially in issue (e.g. the *actio pro socio* or *tutelae* or *fiduciae*).[2] But the context of the sentence is not a recital of the functions of the single judge; it is a minimization of the importance of the *nota censoria*, the judgment made by the censors on the conduct of a citizen. What Cicero is saying is therefore something like this: our ancestors were unwilling that anyone should be a judge, even in a small money dispute (not to speak of judging a man's honour or lack of it), unless the parties had agreed on him as umpire. Note that what Cicero is aiming at, rhetorically, is a contrast between important and unimportant matters; but if that alone had been his object, he could have chosen (as he did elsewhere),[3] as an instance of something notoriously trivial and cognizable by a single judge, an action about *stillicidium*. What he actually produces—or so the passage strikes me—is an instance which combines triviality (*res minima*) with the element of the commonplace (*res pecuniaria*).

The 'money' side of the *unus iudex* is perhaps in this passage no more than glimpsed. A report of Suetonius, however, which deals with only a slightly later era, is stronger evidence; his account[4] of the addition by Augustus of a fourth panel of judges to the three already existing: *quartam addidit ex inferiore censu, quae iudicaret de levioribus summis*. Note that although the *unus iudex* is still the judge of boundaries, ownership, status,

[1] *Pro Cluentio* 120.
[2] See above, p. 95.
[3] *Orator* 72.
[4] *Augustus* 32.

etc., the thing which sticks in the historian's mind as distinguishing this extra panel is that the judges' jurisdiction is limited by reference to the size of money issues before them (*summae*).[1] Of course it is conceivable that the word ought to be understood as referring to the amount of the possible *condemnatio pecuniaria*, but it seems more natural to take its meaning at face value, without paraphrase, and to look at the judges in this panel as presiding over what was essentially a 'Small Claims Court'.[2]

There is also a text of Pliny, already mentioned in a different context,[3] which is absolutely unambiguous in the direction I am suggesting, i.e. the typical association of the *unus iudex* and the *iudicium privatum* with money and, in particular, with business; he describes his own performance in a big centumviral hearing—evidently on a *querela inofficiosi testamenti*—but says: *Intervenit enim acribus illis et erectis*[4] *frequens necessitas computandi ac paene calculos tabulamque poscendi, ut repente in privati iudicii formam centumvirale vertatur.* Nothing could be clearer than this. He is not, of course, saying that a *privatum iudicium* never was concerned with anything but pecuniary disputes, but what he is undoubtedly saying is that the intrusion, into a centumviral trial, of accounting work, almost requiring an account-book and reckoning-aids, instantly suggested the business-like atmosphere—uninteresting to the orator[5]—of a *iudicium privatum* heard by an *unus iudex*.

This passage from Pliny is so much to the point that it scarcely needs the addition of any further text to show the typical, if not exclusive association of the *unus iudex* with money and business. One more hint may, however, be worth quoting: from the well-known passage in Aulus Gellius where he describes his own rather futile efforts as a judge in a *causa pecuniaria*.[6] When he first appeared on the panel of judges for the

[1] *Summa* in the sense of 'sum of money' is common enough in the usage of the Empire.

[2] Cf. the jurisdiction under 36 Geo. III c. 25 (Ir.), 1796, of 'Assistant Barristers', appointed as assistants to the justices of Quarter Sessions: they were empowered to try civil bill proceedings involving not more than £20 in cases of debt.

[3] *Ep.* 6. 33. 9.

[4] The context shows that *illis* refers to something like rhetorical ploys.

[5] See above, pp. 35 ff.

[6] *N.A.* 14. 2. 2.

trial of *iudicia privata*, he says, he looked up whatever law-books he could find on the subject of a judge's duties. But, he says, although I got lots of information on technicalities like the rules of adjournment, I could find nothing to help me *in his autem, quae existere solent, negotiorum ambagibus*—i.e. in regard to the obscurities which tend to arise in business transactions. Now admittedly *negotium* is a word which has meanings wider than 'business transaction', but certainly this is its common meaning in Cicero and later, and it is a far more probable interpretation of it in this context (Gellius goes on to describe an action on an alleged loan) than anything which would be broad enough to take in, for example, the *actio familiae erciscundae* or actions on *stillicidium* or on status.

To summarize my view on the evidence of these texts, then, the single judge is typically engaged in deciding money claims, especially those arising in business. The other areas of his jurisdiction are without the dimension of public interest which would leave them in the field of *recuperatores* or *centumviri*, and are in any case quantitatively insignificant compared with the decision of *causae pecuniariae*. These are essentially claims in contract;[1] and if we recur to the statistical picture built up in the third chapter, it will be seen that these claims enormously preponderate in the second large category of litigation, and preponderate very largely even when those cases are added from the first group which, at any rate in the late Republic, would have been cognizable by an *unus iudex* rather than by a collegiate court.

Without disregarding this minority of 'non-business' cases in which the *unus iudex* was competent, I think it is permissible, in trying to grasp the essence of the institution, to concentrate on what is typical rather than what is secondary, or at any rate quantitatively much less significant. If we do that, the *unus iudex* now stands forth, admittedly in a crude delineation, as the judge of financial or commercial transactions who can try the issue presented to him in the decent privacy of his own house.

[1] Though not exclusively; Cicero says (*Pro Tullio* 5) *nam cum esset de re pecuniaria controversia, quod damnum datum M. Tullio diceremus*...

There remains for consideration the element of the judicial *disposition* in the case of the single judge. What kind of man was he supposed to be, and how was he expected to act in deciding *iudicia privata*? With this question we are at the heart of a phenomenon no less social than legal.

With regard to the first question, although Roman literature contains many hints of improper behaviour on the part even of a single judge,[1] the notion, at least, of the *unus iudex* implied the highest respectability, and the enjoyment of the deserved confidence of others. Two passages from Cicero's speech *pro Roscio Comoedo* make this sufficiently clear, even when all allowances are made for the advocate's interest in flattering the single judge (C. Piso) before whom he was speaking. The former passage is a litany of praise of the judge himself, the defendant, and the counsel involved (the '*advocatio*') who are so distinguished that they deserve as much respect as a single judge does: *quam propter eximium splendorem ut iudicem unum vereri debeamus.*[2] Later in the speech the question arises of the evidence of one who had previously sat as a judge in a case involving Roscius' opponent. Of this former judge, Cluvius, Cicero says:[3] *quem tu si ex censu spectas, eques Romanus est; si ex vita, homo clarissimus est; si ex fide, iudicem sumpsisti* . . . Cicero is concerned to heighten the credit of Cluvius, and invites consideration of him under several aspects, in all of which he scores top marks. 'As to his substance, he belongs to the most well-to-do class; as to his mode of life, it is of the greatest distinction; as to the trust he inspires, his own honour, you yourself, after all, accepted him as judge.' All this is mirrored in the concept of the judge being agreed on between the parties; naturally, it is a mark of high esteem if litigants, bitterly opposed to one another on an issue important to both, can accept him as likely to do his honourable best in deciding their difference.

The idea that the *unus iudex* was the product of agreement between the parties—whether in the sense that they suggested him right from the start, from inside or outside the official

[1] See Kelly, *Roman Litigation*, chs. 2 and 5.

[2] *Pro Roscio Comoedo* 15.

[3] *Ibid.* 42.

roll of judges, or in the sense that the magistrate went on proposing names until the parties heard one whom neither wanted to reject—is treated with reserve if not disfavour by modern writers; it was a significant element in the whole conception of private litigation being based on contract—the doctrine of Wlassak and Wenger—and naturally has to be played down by those who reject the Wlassak theory. Yet it is very hard to ignore the plain message of a well-known Cicero passage in the speech *pro Cluentio*, and the alternative interpretations placed on it, for instance, by Broggini, Kaser, and Behrends are I think very weak. The passage, once again, reads: *Neminem voluerunt maiores nostri non modo de existimatione cuiusquam, sed ne pecuniaria quidem de re minima esse iudicem, nisi qui inter adversarios convenisset.*[1] The question whether or not the Roman formulary trial had a contractual basis is not in itself of any concern to me, but inasmuch as the demolition of the Wlassak position has involved brushing aside this passage as a gross exaggeration, and inasmuch as the issue whether the *unus iudex* was, at any rate originally, someone enjoying the agreed confidence of both sides, is very material to understanding the flavour and quality of the *unus iudex* as a social and legal phenomenon, the arguments used to minimize the *pro Cluentio* evidence must be looked at.

Broggini[2]—one of those who have been foremost in undermining the theory of *litis contestatio* as a contract—gets rid of the inconveniences of the passage as follows: Cicero is aiming at a contrast between the *nota censoria* and *all* judicial trials, criminal as well as civil (notwithstanding that, as Broggini himself admits, *inter adversarios* suggests civil trials only). But if so, to interpret the passage literally would lead to the impossible conclusion that no one could be tried on a criminal charge before a *quaestio* unless he had agreed to the personnel of the court. On the other hand, if indeed he had only civil cases in mind, the passage is a rhetorical failure, because cases involving status (*de capite*) would have been even more important than cases involving reputation (*de existimatione*), and *caput*

[1] *Pro Cluentio* 120.

[2] Op. cit. 55 ff.

cases are not mentioned. To me the possibility that Cicero missed a slight rhetorical trick would fall far short of discrediting the evidence which the passage seems to provide. Broggini concludes that no more can be got from the passage than the message that, if the parties were agreed on a judge, the praetor could not force a different judge on them; he rejects as 'unrealistic' the idea that no issue could be tried by an *unus iudex* unless the parties were agreed on who he was to be. But again, it is only unrealistic if one supposes that a plaintiff who could not get a defendant to agree on a judge was helpless; in fact, pressure both legal and censorial could be brought to bear to ensure that the defendant did agree.[1] Moreover, Cicero is not saying 'no private trial takes place without agreement between the parties on a judge', he is merely saying that 'it was the traditional aim to ensure that there would be no trial without such agreement'—a rather different thing, permitting (for the benefit of the anti-Wlassak school) the inference that this grand old ideal had to be departed from in practice, but leaving intact what is important for my present purpose, namely that such an ideal existed, whether always fully realized or not, and showing that the *unus iudex* as a social phenomenon was embedded in a complex of notions like honour, respectability, and doing things decently.

Kaser[2] regards the *pro Cluentio* passage as an exaggeration, but does not detail his views beyond referring to the view of Broggini just described; the same is true of Jahr.[3] Behrends,[4] however, attacks the passage in a different way; according to him, Cicero himself demonstrates how little trust is to be placed in a literal interpretation of these words, because he gives an account[5] of a proceeding in which there were *quinque iudicibus, nulla lege, nullo instituto, nulla reiectione, nulla sorte ex libidine istius datis*. This means, he says, that in fact an action did take place without any chance being given to the defendant to object to a judge or judges; and so *convenire* in *pro Cluentio* is to be taken

[1] See Kelly, *Roman Litigation*, 25 ff., on the effect of refusal to agree (*recusare*).
[2] *RZPrR* 43 n. 27.
[3] *Litis contestatio*, 111–12.
[4] Op. cit. 49 n. 10.
[5] *Verr.* 2. 2. 41.

as an exaggerated expression for a consent implied from the absence of objection. But—if I have correctly understood Behrends's reasoning—this passage makes it clear that the appointment of the judges was an example of Verres' misbehaviour; in part, this lay in the very fact that *his* whim (*ex libidine istius*) rather than the wishes of the parties dictated the choice of judges; so that, if anything, this text about Verres reinforces rather than weakens the message of *pro Cluentio*. In any case the relevance of the trial set up by Verres to what we are talking about is very doubtful; in *pro Cluentio* Cicero is evidently (from the reference to a *res minima pecuniaria*) talking primarily if not solely about the *unus iudex*, while the five-judge bench appointed by Verres in Sicily is a quite different jurisdiction, probably recuperatorial, though Cicero calls them *iudices*.

To what extent the principle of voluntary agreement on a single judge was upheld, or for how long, or what inroads were made on it (either by way of forcing agreement from a defendant inclined to be recalcitrant, or by way of assigning a judge whom he did not want), are questions that do not affect the dimension of the *unus iudex* revealed by *pro Cluentio* and *pro Roscio Comoedo*. This dimension—the honorific implication of being a single judge enjoying the confidence of parties who can agree, perhaps, on nothing except their common trust of the man who is to settle their difference—is to be added to those already elaborated: the 'private', in the full sense, nature of the litigation he conducts, and the preponderant part played in his jurisdiction by cases about money, particularly business cases. It remains to add the final dimension: the disposition of the *unus iudex* in the actual conduct of the proceedings.

This, in my view, is characterized by an anxiety to see the dispute settled rather than concluded by judgment—an anxiety which the praetorian alternative imperatives *condemnato/absolvito* do not reveal, and which, so far as the words of the formula are concerned, is only distantly hinted at in those actions which contain the so-called *clausula arbitraria*. The conception of the Roman civil procedure as being strongly informed by the spirit of trying to patch up differences rather than flog them to the bitter end of final judgment is not new,[1] but it is worth bringing it into emphasis once more in conjunction with the other facets of the *unus iudex* which I have tried to uncover in this chapter.

In the large class of actions which carried the so-called *clausula arbitraria* it is clear from the fact of the formula itself that the judicial office was directed, not—as some writers put it[2]—to securing 'real' performance for which, in the circumstances, a pecuniary condemnation would have been an unacceptable substitute—but to arriving at a satisfaction of the plaintiff (if the judge thought him in the right) by persuading the defendant to hand over the object in question without the disagreeable preliminary of a condemnation. The formula[3] read as a direction to condemn or absolve, but the condemnation was conditional; it was to take place only if *neque ea res arbitrio* (*iudicis*) *restituetur* (*exhibebitur*, etc.), or words to that effect, and the sense clearly was that the judge, having made up his mind that the merits were on the side of the plaintiff, said so[4] but gave the defendant an opportunity to hand over or produce the thing in question, thus avoiding condemnation, which was pronounced only if he failed to do so. Gaius puts it like this:[5]

> Namque si arbitrum postulaverit is cum quo agitur, accipit formulam quae appellatur arbitraria, et iudicis arbitrio si quid restitui vel exhiberi debeat, id sine periculo exhibet aut restituit, et ita absolvitur; quodsi nec restituat neque exhibeat, quanti ea res est condemnatur. . . . Potius . . . ut modestiore via litiget arbitrum quisque petit quam quia confitetur.

Notice here that—entirely in keeping with the conception of the legal order recognizing the wish not to have something litigated to the bitter end—it is the defendant, not the plaintiff, who is seen as the party who typically asks for the single judge to be classed as an *arbiter*, with an action framed in a *formula arbitraria*; it is in the defendant's interest, if the case is going

[1] See above all Düll, *Der Gütegedanke im römischen Zivilprozessrecht*.

[2] e.g. Kaser, *RZPrR* 257.

[3] Kaser, *RZPrR* 258.

[4] As Gellius (*N.A.* 14. 2) might have done, and Q. Naso in Cicero *Pro Flacco* 50 actually did: *qui cum sententiam secundum Plotium* [the defendant] *se dicturum ostenderet, ab eo iudice abiit* [the plaintiff] *et, quod iudicium lege non erat, causam totam reliquit.*

[5] *Inst.* 4. 163.

against him, to save something from the wreck in the sense of at least avoiding condemnation; to have the case tried at a lower pitch, or more discreetly, more respectably (*modestiore via*) than if this escape-route were not present.

Notice, also, that in this passage of Gaius there is no trace at all of what is supposed[1] to be an inherent part of the machinery of the *formula arbitraria*: the pressurizing of the defendant into surrendering the plaintiff's property by means of the threat of an inflated *condemnatio* based on a deliberately exaggerated, unilateral valuation of the thing by the plaintiff. Gaius simply says that, in the event of non-compliance with an adverse *arbitrium*, the defendant is condemned in the (ordinary) value of the thing: *quanti ea res est*. It is true that there are some texts in the Digest which distinctly say that an inflated judgment, based on the plaintiff's *iusiurandum in litem*, existed in order to penalize the contumacy of a defendant who failed to restore the plaintiff's property;[2] but, quite apart from the question whether these passages are genuine, one of them seems to me to show clearly that the 'penal' element in the judgment was a late arrival and an uncertain one. This is D. 12. 3. 8 (Marcellus):

Tutor rem adulti, quam possidet, restituere ei non vult: quaero, utrum quanti res est an quanti in litem iuratum fuerit condemnari debet. respondi: non est aequum pretio, id est quanti res est, litem aestimari, cum et contumacia punienda sit et arbitrio potius domini rei pretium statuendum sit. . . .

We have already seen[3] that questions reported in the Digest as having been settled by a *responsum* were not speculative or pedagogic exercises, but real litigants' problems. It seems to me inconceivable that, if penality had always been a feature of the *formula arbitraria*—in other words, if the peaceful yielding of the defendant had been not so much in mind as the indirect compulsion of him by means of an unrealistic 'valuation' where he did not yield—this matter could possibly still have been a doubtful issue by the time of Marcellus. If Marcellus is consulted on whether the defendant is to pay *quanti res est* (as his

[1] See, e.g., Kaser, *RZPrR* 259 ff.

[2] D. 4. 3. 18. pr., 12. 3. 1, 2, 8; see also D. 6. 1. 70, 25. 2. 9.

[3] Above, pp. 75 ff.

approximate contemporary Gaius says) or something more, surely this is evidence that the convention of an inflated valuation, with penal intent, can have been only at the point of birth in the second century A.D.; and, arguing back from this, that there was no penal valuation in an earlier era, when the *formula arbitraria* was seen as the *modestior via* in litigation—less injurious to the defendant who was willing to abide by the *arbitrium*—in other words, where the legal system visualized primarily the peaceful rather than the painful outcome of the dispute. Moreover, if the policy behind real actions had always been 'penal' in the sense supposed, it would surely have been a neater and clearer solution to punish contumacy by an express multiple, e.g. double the value, as in some cases of *infitiatio*,[1] rather than by a process comparable with the reverse of what used to be called 'pious perjury'.[2]

However, the association of the single judge with the respectable, discreet settlement of disputes does not stop with the *formula arbitraria*. It seems to me that there is evidence that even in actions not equipped with the formal possibility of avoiding condemnation by obeying the *arbitrium*, the judge was empowered and even expected to try to help the parties to arrive at a settlement and in that way to avoid a condemnation (where the merits were against the defendant). This evidence lies in a few texts from the late Republic and early Empire. The best-known is probably Cicero's description, in the *pro Caecina*,[3] of the tardiness which characterized judgments where the standing (*existimatio*) of the defendant was at stake, as of course it would be in a very large number of actions, even if not technically *actiones famosae*. Cicero says the *recuperatores* had twice delayed a final decision, not because of doubt as to the rights and wrongs, but *quod videtur ad summam illius existimationem hoc iudicium pertinere, moram ad condemnandum acquisisse, simul et illi spatium ad sese colligendum dedisse. quod quoniam iam in*

[1] In, e.g., the *actio iudicati* or *legis Aquiliae*.

[2] Whereby, in order to avert a capital sentence on a person convicted of theft, a jury would swear that the stolen goods were worth less than forty shillings (the level above which a capital sentence was passed), irrespective of the true value of the goods.

[3] 6.

*consuetudinem venit, et id viri boni, vestri similes, in iudicando faciunt . . .* If a condemnation was inevitable in the end, what was to be gained for anyone by delaying it and giving the defendant time *ad sese colligendum*, unless he was to put this time to use by satisfying the plaintiff or settling with him? And if this was so in a recuperatorial trial, which as we have seen was a 'tough' form of proceeding, tending to bruise the defendant by its very initiation, let alone its outcome, it must have been all the more noticeable in the more gentlemanly atmosphere of the single-judge trial. Then there is a case reported by Valerius Maximus[1] about an action to recover a dowry which was heard by Marius in public;[2] after the hearing had begun, Marius took the plaintiff privately aside and tried to persuade him to restore the woman's dowry: . . . *seductum Titinium monuit ut incepto desisteret ac mulieri dotem redderet. Quod cum saepius frustra fecisset, coactus ab eo sententiam pronuntiare . . .* His efforts to dissuade Titinius from the course of greed were in vain, and in the end he had no other course than to pronounce judgment against him. In other words, judgment might have been averted if Titinius had followed the judge's informal attempts to settle the matter peaceably.

This little anecdote gives, I think, a sense to a further passage —from Horace, an older contemporary of Valerius Maximus— which has not previously been attributed to it. The passage[3] is the reply to the imaginary question, *Vir bonus est quis?* and reads:

> qui consulta patrum, qui leges iuraque servat,
> quo multae magnaeque secantur iudice lites,
> quo res sponsore et quo causae teste tenentur.

This model citizen is usually understood[4] as being praised for having given judgment in many serious cases, but on reflection it seems to me that this sense is too thin; the judgments, after

[1] 8. 2. 3.

[2] *In conspectu habita quaestione*: perhaps it means no more than 'in the presence of others' in the sense of the parties' witnesses, his own *consilium* etc., rather than 'in a public place', 'open to the world'.

[3] *Ep.* I. 16. 42.

[4] e.g. by the lexicographers, who take *secare* here to mean 'decide'.

all, might be bad ones. More likely is the reading which would take *secantur* as meaning, not 'decided', but 'cut short', and the good man deserves praise because he has, through his good offices, put an end to many serious disputes by using his position as judge to get the parties to settle. There is, lastly, a discussion reported from Aulus Gellius about the propriety of a judge interfering to secure a settlement after he has heard the case—rather like Marius in the tale of Valerius Maximus—and from Gellius' words[1] it is obvious that the discussion concerns an actual practice, not a suggested one: *Id etiam . . . quaeri solet, an deceat atque conveniat iudici causa iam cognita, si facultas esse videatur conponendi negotii, officio paulisper iudicis dilato communis amicitiae et quasi pacificatoria partis recipere?*

[1] *N.A.* 14. 2. 15.

# CONCLUSION

THE results which I hope I may have obtained in the five chapters of this short book vary substantially in hardness. Some conclusions—for example about the far-from-marginal position of the *centumviri*, or the coercive aspect of the recuperatorial jurisdiction—seem to me persuasive enough. Others—for example as to the relationship between the composition of the *centumviri* and the *ius gentilicium*—I offer merely as hypotheses. Others I can scarcely even describe as hypotheses; rather as impressionistic presentations of phenomena from somewhat different perspectives than those usual up to now. Over all, I have tried to suggest that the Republican judicature, so far from being the haphazard assortment of jurisdictions which a reading of the textbooks and monographs might imply, was a reasonably well articulated scheme, each of its three principal arms having its own field of operation for its own social or legal reasons.[1] I am conscious that the figure of the *unus iudex*, who looms in the textbooks high above the others, has received from me the most impressionistic treatment of the three; and I would conclude these short studies by trying to indicate concisely how I visualize his rather special aura.

His activity—as shown by the extreme numerical disparity between one and a hundred—was private; it was honourable; it carried a distinct flavour of the 'decent', 'respectable' composition of what, if not so treated, would be disagreeable and embarrassing squabbles; it was largely about money disputes

[1] Professor Kunkel comments privately that he is not convinced that in the Republic there was such a thing as an 'exclusive' civil competence in any court, and wonders whether e.g. within certain limits an area of choice existed as to whether an action would be tried by the *centumviri* or by an *unus iudex*; and thinks, in general, that jurisdictional organs originating at different times and in different circumstances might conceivably have had a degree of overlapping competence. This possibility cannot be ignored, but it seems to me legitimate to start from the assumption of principle that different organs were meant to have different functions, and that the burden of proof, so to speak, lies on anyone asserting that different organs might have had the same function.

and, specifically, those arising in business; it was informed by the spirit of arbitration agreed by both parties and so did not normally find itself on the plane of coercion or the overbearing of recalcitrance, by contrast with the recuperatorial jurisdiction; by contrast with that of the *centumviri*, it concerned matters which the public policy of the Romans was content not to drag forth into the gaze of those whom they did not affect.

If this sketch of the *unus iudex* is accurate, it seems to me highly unlikely that he is a figure as old as the Roman legal order itself, despite his appearance in the XII Tables. Admittedly the XII Tables commonly rank as the first milestone in Roman legal history, but this code itself contains clear signs of more archaic strata; and it seems to me that some of the aspects of the *unus iudex*, as he appears in the late Republic, argue a more sophisticated, more commercially oriented, more 'gentlemanly' society than that which was trying to say goodbye to *talio*, and which enforced attendance of witnesses by the ritual *obvagulatio*. As to the question, then, whether or not the *unus iudex* is an aboriginal figure on the Roman judicial scene, I would answer it by saying that some kind of single judge may quite possibly go back well beyond the XII Tables, whether as someone to whom the king or magistrate delegated judicial power, or as someone whose choice by the parties was officially endorsed; but that the *unus iudex* of the late Republic is embedded in a set of social ideas which it is hard to imagine flourishing in the modest, agriculture-oriented society of the fifth century B.C., and these ideas are so central to his conception as to make him quite a different creature from an *unus iudex* operating half a millennium before.

The *recuperatores*, on the other hand—the 'recoverers', 'enforcers'—must represent the Roman Republic's first move to assure the regular operation of the law against those who were impervious to disrepute or social pressure or the plaintiff's own efforts. As such, they must belong to an era well after the XII Tables, which knew nothing of supplementary remedies (of the kind later developed by the praetor) to shore up the legal process or the litigating of *furtum* or *iniuria* against bullies.

The *centumviri*—to end with my starting-point—are perhaps best visualized as an ancient representative assembly of a kin-organized people, whose legislative functions are petrified or exercised by others, but which retains, in judicial shape, the supervision of large issues involving succession to family property and thus to the material base for family survival.

This statement of my conception of the Republic's judicial complex is offered, not as the last word, but as the first, in a long-overdue discussion.

# INDEX OF SOURCES

## I. LEGAL SOURCES


Gaius, *Institutiones*
1. 119 — 24
3. 12 — 20
3. 216 — 109
4. 14 — 56
4. 16 — 7, 14, 31
4. 17a — 104, 121
4. 30 — 27
4. 31 — 6, 27, 33
4. 32 — 52
4. 48 — 29
4. 95 — 6, 14, 33
4. 104 — 7
4. 105 — 58, 61 ff.
4. 109 — 62
4. 163 — 129
4. 182 — 63, 95

*Codex Theodosianus*
1. 12. 1 — 110
1. 16. 9 — 110

*Justiniani Digesta* (*not* including the groups of passages mentioned only for statistical purposes, pp. 79–88, q.v.)
1. 2. 2. 2 — 21
1. 2. 2. 29 — 12, 67
1. 2. 2. 30 — 68
1. 2. 2. 49 — 76
2. 11. 4 pr. — 77
3. 3. 46. 4 — 16
3. 5. 25 (26) — 80
4. 3. 18 pr. — 130
5. 2. 13 — 14
5. 2. 17 pr. — 14
5. 3 — 15
5. 4 — 15
5. 4. 10 — 77
6. 1. 70 — 130
8. 2. 10 — 14
8. 2. 31 — 14
8. 4. 16 — 14
9. 2. 2. 1 — 109
9. 2. 23. 10 — 109
9. 2. 33 pr. — 32–3
9. 3. 5. 12 — 77
12. 3. 1, 2, 8 — 130
15. 1. 38. 1 — 77
15. 1. 50 pr. — 16
17. 1. 54 — 32
17. 1. 59. 4 — 81
17. 2. 52. 18 — 16
20. 5. 12. 1 — 16, 77
21. 2. 39 pr. — 108
23. 3. 71 — 77
25. 2. 9 — 130
28. 1. 3 — 116
28. 2. 2 — 77
28. 6. 25 — 77
35. 2. 87. 3 — 77
39. 4. 1 pr. — 52
40. 1. 24 pr. — 11
40. 4. 48 — 77
40. 5. 26. 7 — 56
40. 5. 26. 10 — 56
40. 7. 29. 1 — 16
40. 12. 30 — 13
42. 1 — 65
42. 1. 4. 3 — 65
42. 1. 4. 8 — 65
42. 1. 5. 1 — 65
42. 1. 11 — 65
42. 1. 12 — 65
42. 1. 15. 2 ff. — 65
42. 1. 16 — 65
42. 1. 20 — 65
42. 1. 30 — 65
42. 1. 36 — 12
42. 1. 38 — 11
42. 1. 52 — 65
42. 1. 64 — 65
44. 1. 16–18 — 13
46. 1. 67 — 16
46. 8. 22. 4 — 16
47. 10 — 93, 95
47. 10. 15. 25 — 102
47. 10. 15. 32 — 64
47. 10. 19 — 64, 100
50. 17. 85 pr. — 77

*Justiniani institutiones*
4. 16 pr. — 96

*Pauli Sententiae*
5. 9. 1 — 16

## II. NON-LEGAL SOURCES


*Cato*
or. frg. (Ford) 56 113
*Catullus*
68. 119 ff. 25
*Cicero*
Epistulae
ad Att.
2. 4. 1 97
5. 21. 10 69
ad fam.
9. 21. 1 111, 114
Orationes
in Caec. divin.
18 113
55 ff. 57–8, 69
pro Caecina
6 120, 131
7–8 63
8 119, 121
9 64
14 99
23 60, 99
26 61
28 60
61 119
93 99
97 67
pro Cluentio
74 114
120 122, 126
163 113–14
de domo sua
78 68
108 113–14
pro Flacco
12 113–14
50 129
de har. resp. 14, 16 113
de l. agraria
2. 44 14
pro Murena
11 99
27 118
pro Quinctio
5 99
9 99
11 99
12 99
14 99
21 99
22 99
22 99
26 99
30 99
38 99
46 99
48 99
53 99, 109
56 99
79 99
pro Q. Rosc.
16 113–14
24–5 114
pro Rosc. Com.
4 99
15 125
20 99
42 125
post red. in sen.
21 114
pro Tullio
3, 5 102
in Verr.
2. 1. 73–4 69
2. 1. 115 25
2. 1. 146 28
2. 2. 41 127
2. 2. 71 114
2. 2. 75 113–14
2. 3. 35 51
2. 3. 135, 138 119
[Rhet ad Her.]
1. 8 99
1. 12. 22 113
1. 13. 23 20
2. 13. 19 63, 100
4. 36. 48 113
Philosophica
de leg. 3. 8 105
de off. 2. 64 97
de rep. 2. 14 21
de sen. 21 113
Tusc. quaest. 3. 5. 11 20
Rhetorica
Brutus
84 104
144 14
177 114
178 113
197 14, 35
217 113–14
238 113–14

Rhetorica, Brutus (*cont.*):
245–6 113–14
311–12 113–14
322 114
de invent.
1. 3–4 114
1. 11–12 113
1. 22 99
1. 35 113
1. 38 113
2. 58 114
2. 92 113
de opt. gen. or.
4. 10–11 111, 114–15
orator
72 39, 111, 115, 122
129 113
de oratore
1. 173 6, 9 ff., 14, 20, 35, 114, 116
1. 176 20, 24, 25
1. 178–9 114
1. 181 10
1. 202 114
1. 238 10
2. 98 36
2. 100 114
2. 105 108
2. 172 96
3. 212 111
part. or. 29. 102. 108
topica 17. 65 114
*Dio Cassius*
54. 26. 6–7 67–8
*Dion. Hal.*
2. 7 21
*Festus*
de verb. sign.
(ed. Mueller)
42 21, 23
54 3, 7–8, 22 ff.
276 42
*Gellius*
Noctes Atticae
2. 23. 8 32
5. 13. 6 96
7. 6. 10 113
11. 18. 18 113
13. 12. 6–7 58, 69, 113
14. 2 99, 110, 113–14, 123, 129, 133
16. 10. 8 6, 27
17. 2. 10 104
20. 1. 7 5
*Hieronymus*
ep. 50. 2 14
*Horace*
ars poetica 131 113
ep. 1. 16. 42 132
*Juvenal*
sat. 7. 115 ff. 39, 54
*Livy*
1. 13. 6 21
2. 54. 7 113
2. 55. 8 113
3. 55. 7 107
3. 55. 7 66, 69
3. 71 ff. 46
25. 18. 5, 9 113
26. 48. 8 44
29. 16–21 45
32. 10 46
34. 2. 10 113
39. 3. 1 45
39. 18. 6 113
43. 2 44
*Macrobius*
Saturn. 3. 16. 15 16, 104, 106
*Martial*
6. 19 39
6. 38. 5 35, 38
7. 63. 7 38
10. 19 (20). 15 38
*Nepos*
Atticus 6. 3 97
Themist. 1. 3 114
*Ovid*
Pont. 3. 5. 21 ff. 38
Trist. 2. 95 114
*Phaedrus*
fab. 3. 10 14
*Plautus*
Bacch. 270 41, 47
Capt.
334–5 113
775 31
Curc. 552 113
Men. 580 ff. 5
Poen. 1403 ff. 47
Rud. 1282 41, 47
Trin.
38 113
287 113
484 31
*Pliny* (senior)
n.h. 36. 2. 5–6 28
*Pliny* (junior)
ep. 1. 18. 3 36

*Pliny* (junior) (*cont.*):
2. 14. 1 17
2. 14. 4 ff. 35
4. 24. 1 36
5. 1. 7 14
6. 12. 2 36
6. 33. 3 11, 35, 36, 116
6. 33. 7–9 114, 115, 123
8. 18. 4 108
*Plutarch*
Rom. 14 21
*Probus*
de litt. sing. frg.
5. 8 60
*Quintilian*
decl. 266 114
inst. or.
3. 10. 3 14
4. 1. 57 111
4. 2. 5 14
4. 2. 9 102
4. 2. 61–2 114
5. 7. 26 102
5. 10. 114 114
5. 10. 115 111, 114
6. 2. 23 96
6. 4. 7 114
7. 2. 28 102
7. 4. 20 14
11. 3. 150 114
12. 5. 6 36
*Seneca* (senior)
contr.
9 praef. 3 110
7. 1 (16). 22 114
7. 2 (17). 7–8 114
*Seneca* (junior)
de benef. 2. 8. 2 98
de clem. 1. 9–10 114
de ira
2. 9. 1–4 108
3. 33. 1–2 110
*Statius*
Silv.
1. 4. 24 38
4. 4. 39 ff. 38
4. 9. 16 38
*Suetonius*
Div. Jul.
1. 2 25
18 113
Aug.
29 107
32 122
36 67
Tib. 33 109
Claud. 14 114
Vesp. 10 37
frg. (Roth) 290. 10 ff. 37
rhet. 30 35
*Tacitus*
Ann.
1. 75 109
14. 28. 4 114
Dial.
38 36
40 101
*Valerius Maximus*
7. 7. 1 14, 36
7. 7. 2 14
7. 8. 7 114
8. 2. 2 113
8. 2. 3 132
*Varro*
de ling. lat.
5. 4. 2 113
6. 86 113
6. 91–2 113
9. 68 113
res rust.
2. 1. 26 3, 7
3, 2, 1 113
*Vitruvius*
de archit.
6. 5. 2 110, 114

## III. LEGES, EPIGRAPHIC SOURCES

*CIL* 10. 5917 = Dessau 1909 68
14. 3492 = Dessau 1938 68
Dessau 1911 68
fragm. Atestinum 51
'Laudatio Turiae' (= Dessau 8393) 13 ff. 20
lex agraria 30, 34, 35 50
lex Antonia de Termessibus 48 ff., 55
lex XII Tabularum 7a 20
lex Lat. tab. Bant. 9 ff. 50
lex Mamilia 59
lex Ursonensis 51, 59, 61, 113

# INDEX OF CONTENTS


*adoptio*, 24–5
*adrogatio*, 24–5
*centumviri*, 2 ff.
  antiquity, 5 ff.
  composition, 3 ff., 22 ff.
  *hasta* as emblem, 7, 9, 14
  jurisdiction, 8 ff.
  prominence in forensic life, 34 ff., 91
  reason for special features, 20 ff.
*clausula arbitraria*, 119, 129 ff.
*comitia calata*, 23 ff.
common law, 'quia timet' injunction, 30
*condemnatio/absolutio*, 29
  does not express whole function of *unus iudex*, 128
*condemnatio pecuniaria*, 29 ff.
*cura*, 26–7
*curia*, 20 ff.
*damnum infectum*, 28 ff.
*decemviri stlitibus iudicandis*, 66 ff.
*existimatio*, imperilled by litigation, 96 ff.
*favor libertatis*, 12, 56
*fideicommissa libertas*, 55 ff.
*formula*, formulary procedure, 27 ff.
*gens, gentiles, ius gentilicium*, 20 ff.
*hereditatis petitio*, 14 ff., 30 ff.
*ignominia*, 95 ff.
*infamia*, 95 ff.
inheritance, *see* succession
*iniuria iudicis*, 16
Ireland, district names and family names, 21
  early law on insult, 93 ff.
  pattern of modern litigation, 70 ff.
  specific performance of modern contract, 32
*iudex arbiterve*, 117 ff.
*iudex privatus*, rarity of phrase, 114
  meaning, 115
  see *unus iudex*
*iudicium legitimum/imperio continens*, 7, 61 ff.
*iudicium privatum*, 115, 131
*legis actio*, procedure, 27 ff.
  *sacramento*, 29 ff.
*leges Iuliae*, 27 ff.
*liberalis causa*, 10 ff., 54 ff.
*patria potestas*, devolution of, 33–4
publicity, supposedly normal in litigation, 103 ff.
  in fact no such rule for *iudicia privata*, 110 ff.
*querela inofficiosi testamenti*, 14 ff., 18
*recuperatores*, 1, 12, 13, 17
  competence in delicts involving public danger, 53 ff.
  connection with enforcement of judgments, 47 ff., 65 ff., 69–70
  etymology, 49
  *causae liberales*, 54 ff.
  origin of specialised jurisdiction, 400 ff.
  and *repetundae*, 44 ff.
  share of litigation, 91–2
  speed of procedure, 53–4
  supposed 'international' character, 41 ff., 48
*rescripta*, system of counting and grouping, 85–6
*responsa*, arose in setting of real practice, 75 ff.
  system of counting and grouping, 78 ff.
  usage in *Digest*, 77–8
*sacra*, 25, 31
slaves, slavery, blood relationship with *dominus*, 32–3
statistics of litigation, 71 ff.
status, litigation on, 10, 54 ff.
succession, 14 ff., 20 ff.
  very heavily represented among *responsa* and *rescripta*, 83, 87
  predominant place in litigation, 90
  field of *centumviri*, 14 ff.
*tribus*, 34 ff., 7, 20 ff.
*tutela*, 26–7
*unus iudex*, 17 f., 112 ff.
  agreement on, 122
  disposition to effect settlement, 131 ff.
  'image', 124 ff.
*vindicationes*, 13–14
*vituperatio*, normal forensic practice, 98 ff.
  not ground for *actio iniuriarum*, 100 ff.
*vocatio*, magistral power, 58
witnesses, official summoning of, 58 ff.